T0323824

The Search for Entrepreneurship

Since the 1980s, governments have eagerly encouraged entrepreneurship on the assumption that it creates small businesses which are the primary drivers of job creation. Largely because of this assumption, entrepreneurship has become a valid subject for academic research, attracting extensive funding.

Yet despite this explosion of scholarship, there is no accepted model of how entrepreneurship operates or even a commonly accepted definition of what it is. Simon Bridge posits that this is because entrepreneurship has been studied as if it were a deterministic science, based on the false assumption that it exists as a specific discrete identifiable phenomenon operating in accordance with consistent, predictable 'rules'.

This challenging book contends that this misdirected search has produced more questions than answers. Accepting that entrepreneurship as we have conceived it does not exist could lead to new and valuable insights into what the different forms of entrepreneurship are and how they might be influenced. Scholars, advanced students and policy makers will find this a thought-provoking insight into the nature and scope of entrepreneurship.

Simon Bridge is a visiting Professor at the University of Ulster. His other publications include: *Understanding Enterprise, Entrepreneurship and Small Business* with Ken O'Neill (4th edition 2013, 5th edition forthcoming); *Understanding the Social Economy and the Third Sector* with Brendan Murtagh and Ken O'Neill (2nd edition 2014); *Beyond the Business Plan* with Cecilia Hegarty, (2013); *Rethinking Enterprise Policy: Can failure trigger new understanding?* (2010).

Routledge Focus on Business and Management

The fields of business and management have grown exponentially as areas of research and education. This growth presents challenges for readers trying to keep up with the latest important insights. Routledge Focus on Business and Management presents small books on big topics and how they intersect with the world of business.

Individually, each title in the series provides coverage of a key academic topic, whilst collectively, the series forms a comprehensive collection across the business disciplines.

The Search for Entrepreneurship

Finding More Questions Than Answers

Simon Bridge

Routledge
Taylor & Francis Group

LONDON AND NEW YORK

First published 2017
by Routledge
2 Park Square, Milton Park, Abingdon, Oxon OX14 4RN

and by Routledge
605 Third Avenue, New York, NY 10017

First issued in paperback 2021

Routledge is an imprint of the Taylor & Francis Group, an informa business

Publisher's Note
The publisher has gone to great lengths to ensure the quality of this reprint but points out that some imperfections in the original copies may be apparent.

British Library Cataloguing in Publication Data
A catalogue record for this book is available from the British Library

Library of Congress Cataloging in Publication Data
A catalog record for this book has been requested

ISBN 13: 978-1-03-224231-6 (pbk)
ISBN 13: 978-1-138-29268-0 (hbk)

DOI: 10.4324/9781315232751

Typeset in Times New Roman
by Apex CoVantage, LLC

Contents

Illustrations

Figures

Table

Boxes

Preface

This book is about a search in which in one way or another I have been engaged for over 30 years. It started when I joined a small business agency as its Enterprise Development Director and was tasked with raising 'the propensity of people to create jobs for themselves and others'.[1] Although we then referred to that as 'enterprise', subsequently it has increasingly been labelled 'entrepreneurship' – and I have been exploring it ever since, whether as a policy maker and policy implementer, a consultant and facilitator or, from a rather more detached perspective, as an author and visiting professor.

It might seem strange, after all that time, to conclude that the subject of my search does not actually exist. I may be fortunate or, depending on one's point of view, burdened, in now having the inclination, the freedom and the opportunity to reflect on my journey and to query some of the assumptions I had initially acquired as the apparently relevant knowledge about this field of endeavour. However, increasingly, as I have tried to identify, clarify and substantiate this received wisdom, I have begun to think that much of it did not stand up to close scrutiny. In particular the more I probed the 'entrepreneurship' which had been assumed to exist, the less clear I felt about what it was. The result has been some of the thoughts summarised in this book. It has been a while in its gestation, but it has now emerged, as if at a time of its own choosing.

In all this I owe debts and/or apologies to many people – but there isn't room here to list them, even if I could remember all their names. Nevertheless I would like to single out two people who have helped particularly with contributions and/or critiques for this book – and they are Spinder Dhaliwal and Ken O'Neill. Thank you very much for all your help and encouragement – and if there are any errors or omissions in the final result, it is my fault not yours.

Simon Bridge, Holywood

Note

1 Department of Economic Development, *Building a Stronger Economy: The Pathfinder Process* (Belfast, 1987), p. 11.

Acknowledgments

The author and publisher gratefully acknowledge permission from the following to reproduce copyright material:

- The Office of National Statistics under the Open Government License for the unemployment data used for Figure 1.1
- Norris Krueger for permission to reproduce Figure 7.1 from *Prescription for Opportunity: How Communities Can Create Potential for Entrepreneurs* (Washington, DC: Small Business Foundation of America, Working Paper 93-03, 1995)
- Palgrave Macmillan, under authors' rights to re-use content, for permission to reproduce Table 2.1 and Illustration 4.2 from Simon Bridge, *Rethinking Enterprise Policy*, (Palgrave Macmillan, 2010)
- John Wiley & Sons for permission to reproduce Figure 7.3 from W. J. Dennis, 'Entrepreneurship, Small Business and Public Policy Levers', *Journal of Small Business Management* 49/1, 2011

About the author

Simon Bridge is a visiting Professor at the University of Ulster. After several other jobs, he joined LEDU (Local Enterprise Development Unit – the Northern Ireland government's small business agency) in 1984 where he was the Enterprise Development Director. In 1993, he set up his own business as a consultant and a facilitator of enterprise and voluntary/community-sector development. His clients have included government departments and agencies, district councils, local enterprise agencies, universities and further education institutions, private businesses and many third-sector bodies – and his work for them has included feasibility studies, economic appraisals, business cases, funding applications, project evaluations and, where required, business plans. He has also undertaken assignments in Russia, Ukraine, Slovakia, Bulgaria, Mozambique, Romania, Lithuania and Turkey and served on the boards of several third-sector enterprises. His other publications include: *Understanding Enterprise, Entrepreneurship and Small Business* with Ken O'Neill (4th edition 2013, 5th edition forthcoming); *Understanding the Social Economy and the Third Sector* with Brendan Murtagh and Ken O'Neill (2nd edition 2014); *Beyond the Business Plan* with Cecilia Hegarty, (2013); *Rethinking Enterprise Policy: Can failure trigger new understanding?* (2010).

1   Why?

Why have we been searching for entrepreneurship and why write this book?

The search for entrepreneurship

The first business textbook this author acquired was initially published in 1958, it had the title 'Business Enterprise'[1] and it purported to be 'a study of the economic and political organisation of British industry' and to describe and analyse its variety. However, in looking at the book now, what seems to be particularly noticeable is not what it says but what it doesn't say. For instance, while it does occasionally indicate that some businesses are small and that most businesses start small, nowhere does it treat small businesses as being in any way distinct or worthy of any form of separate consideration. It generally focuses *on* firms and does not dwell a lot on the people behind them. Also, in looking at the birth of firms, it suggests that 'new firms generally do the same sort of things as old ones' and does not consider issues such as 'creative destruction'. The people who start businesses are generally referred to as 'founders', although the person starting from scratch to do something new is referred to as 'an innovator' who is 'generally giving a longer rein to his enthusiasm than to his common sense'[2] and, possibly what is most significant for a book on 'business enterprise', is that it does not appear to use the word 'entrepreneur' at all.

Now, however, that perspective has changed, and business books no longer ignore small businesses and the concepts of enterprise, entrepreneurs and entrepreneurship that are associated with them. As Gibb pointed out in 2000: 'Since the 1980s and particularly into the 1990s there has been an explosion of research into entrepreneurship and the small and medium enterprise' and that 'this is reflected in a substantial growth in both the academic literature and in the grey literature of the press, journals and consultant reports'.[3] As a consequence, as it has seemed to one observer: 'Simply put, there are too many journals for faculty in entrepreneurship today.'[4]

A reflection of that surge in interest can be found in the following observation made in 1992:

> The field [of entrepreneurship] is evolving rapidly with more than 100 endowed academic chairs, over 70 research centers worldwide, and an excess of 25 academic journals. More than 700 papers are presented at conferences annually. Many other complementary activities have arisen, such as entrepreneurs of the year programs, entrepreneurship awareness programs, enterprise forums, and volunteer assistance programs. Today entrepreneurship is a recognized discipline.[5]

And that interest continues. For instance:

- In 2008 a Kauffman Foundation report indicated that more than 5,000 entrepreneurial courses were being offered by colleges and universities in the United States and that in 2013 well over 400,000 students took courses in the subject.[6]
- In 2013 it was reported that since 1990 the numbers of academic papers published on entrepreneurship had grown from fewer than 100 to over 5,000 – an annual growth rate of just over 12 per cent.[7]

Governments also have been very interested in entrepreneurship, not least in response to problems of low economic growth and high unemployment. Examples of entrepreneurship policies or intentions from different countries or even international organisations include the following:

- In 2013 the Welsh Assembly published its policy of economic renewal in which it said that '[t]here remains a role for Government in encouraging entrepreneurship – it is vital for developing a strong economy and therefore crucial for our future prosperity'.[8]
- In 2013 the EU published its Entrepreneurship 2020 Action Plan, the introduction to which indicates that:

> to bring Europe back to growth and create new jobs, we need more entrepreneurs [and that the]. Action Plan . . . is a blueprint for action to unleash Europe's entrepreneurial potential, remove existing obstacles and revolutionize the culture of entrepreneurship in the EU.[9]

- In the United States in 2014 Secretary of State John Kerry stated: 'The United States has learned through its own experience that entrepreneurship is an essential driver of prosperity and freedom.'[10]
- In 2014 the G20 leaders declared that 'to lift growth and create jobs . . . we are promoting competition, entrepreneurship and innovation'.[11]

Although much of this increased government interest may have started as far back as the 1980s, it does not appear subsequently to have diminished and may instead have strengthened further. For instance, in looking at this 'political entrepreneurship', one observer noted in 2015 that:

> In recent years and not least after the latest financial and economic crisis, we have seen a strongly renewed interest for industrial policy to get the developed economies growing again. . . . Politicians and their experts and advisers have been hunting desperately for new approaches to industrial policy . . . publically financed activities that with different methods try to stimulate entrepreneurship and self-employment with the overall goal to increase employment and economic growth.[12]

Why have we been searching for entrepreneurship?

Because of all this interest in entrepreneurship and the associated concepts of enterprise and small businesses, they are now common and popular subjects referred to frequently in many media and often pursued and/or courted. Although the pursuit of them may have been stimulated, and funded, by governments, especially during and after the 1980s, nevertheless, as Gibb observed, it has been particularly prominent in academic and research circles. But what essentially has been sought in this pursuit – and why?

Following the Second World War the economies of countries like the UK seemed to regain some equilibrium following the upheavals of the war and the earlier economic problems of the 1930s. For about 30 years after the war there was relatively low unemployment – and that had even begun to seem like the norm. However, in the 1970s things began to change, as Figure 1.1 illustrates, and, by the end of that decade it was clear that unemployment was rising alarmingly and apparently inexorably and that, not just in the UK, economies were not responding as they had in response to the usual economic controls.

In this alarming situation governments were anxiously looking for new economic solutions, and therefore there was a lot of interest when, in 1979, David Birch released the results of his research into employment in the United States[13] in which he concluded that it was small firms which created the most jobs. As he put it slightly later:

> Of all the net new jobs created in our sample of 5.6 million businesses between 1969 and 1976, two-thirds were created by firms with twenty or fewer employees and about 80 percent were created by firms with 100 or fewer employees.[14]

Birch spoke about net new jobs, which are the difference between the total number of new jobs created and the number of jobs lost during the same

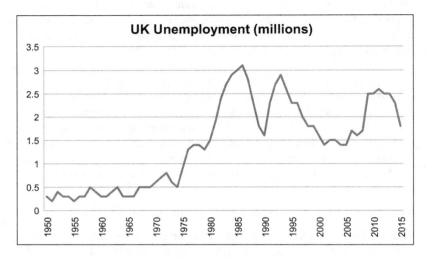

Figure 1.1 UK unemployment 1950–2015

Source: Office for National Statistics, Labour Market Statistics.

period. Birch found that all areas of the United States were losing jobs at more or less the same rate but that some areas were growing economically because they were creating jobs faster than they were losing them. What distinguished higher-growth areas from the others, therefore, was not the rate of job losses but the rate of job replacement by new job creation. As this job creation requires innovation, which involves risk taking and consequently some failures, he concluded that the most successful areas were those with the highest rates of innovation and failure, not the lowest.[15] Net new jobs is sometimes used as a reasonable indicator of economic growth and, because of Birch's finding that it was small firms which were the prime source of this employment creation, the implication was that they were thus responsible for much of the economic growth – at least in the United States.

Many people discounted Birch's work when it was first published, as his conclusion was contrary to the perceived wisdom of that time which was still influenced by Fordism and the supposed economic primacy of big corporations. Nevertheless, the issue was important enough to stimulate others to try to replicate his work, and many years later the statistical debate still continues. Birch's work has been challenged on a number of occasions, with one line being that the age of the firm is important and that it is young businesses, not small ones, which create the most new jobs.[16] But, nevertheless, Birch's work has been very influential and, in the belief that small businesses were going to be the best source of the new jobs they wanted to see being created, governments wanted more small businesses. Further they believed that the businesses they wanted would be created by the enterprise of entrepreneurs – so they wanted more enterprise and more entrepreneurs.

There were, of course, other reasons for wanting more small businesses beyond just the direct contribution of more jobs. Small businesses were understood to fill an important niche in economies, indirectly supporting growth by providing things like innovation, specialist supply and wider choice – and in some cases being the embryo big businesses of the future. By such means they contributed to economic growth, which itself provided not just more jobs but more prosperity – and more tax revenues. Nevertheless employment was a crucial driver, and the policy argument generally relied on a set of assumptions which might be summarised as:

- To reduce unemployment we need more jobs.
- New businesses, most of which will at least start small, create jobs and contribute to economic growth and the benefits it is supposed to bring such as increased prosperity and tax revenues.
- Therefore, we need more new/small businesses.

Sometimes the factor which was supposed to stimulate those new businesses was labelled enterprise, but now that seems to have been largely superseded by the concept of entrepreneurship as the condition which generates and/ or encourages a supply of entrepreneurs who will in turn create the desired new businesses. Thus entrepreneurship became a sort of magic potion – the hoped-for ingredient the application of which could cure economies. And it would appear that many people still see it in this way:

> When policy makers and other observers emphasise the role of entre- preneurship, they almost exclusively focus on its role as a generator of jobs, economic growth and wealth.[17]

When policy makers have budgets to pursue something, that encourages others to join in the pursuit – with the result that many people have been looking for entrepreneurship and entrepreneurs and for ways of influencing them. Because of the policy agenda summarised earlier, we want to know what entrepreneurs are, where they can be found, how we can recognise them and what stimulates then – and we want to know that so that we can develop more of them and encourage those that we have to do more. It has even been suggested that we also want this research to show why it is being undertaken by identifying the value of the 'entrepreneurship' that policy has decided to pursue:

> From the 1980s there has been a considerable political and policy *demand* for research showing the value of entrepreneurs to the econ-

omy, to rationalize political decisions that have already been taken and guide future policy making.[18]

The search and its results

The result is that entrepreneurship has emerged as a popular subject and that a search for it has, in many countries, been initiated, prompted largely by government policy in pursuit of more economic development and in particular more employment. In the apparent belief that more entrepreneurship means more entrepreneurs creating more new businesses which will in turn create more jobs and more wealth, governments have wanted more entrepreneurship. Therefore, they have wanted to know what entrepreneurship is and what triggers, stimulates and/or encourages it on the assumption that they will then be able to use that knowledge to get more of it. The implication is that entrepreneurship has been sought on the assumption that it is a condition which causes more entrepreneurs to emerge who will in turn have the effect of starting more businesses and employing more people.

Consequently there have been attempts to treat entrepreneurship as a deterministic science like physics and to harness it like electricity to a useful purpose. However, such thinking depends on the two assumptions that entrepreneurship exists as a specific discrete identifiable phenomenon and that it operates in accordance with 'rules' in a consistent and predictable way – and it is the contention of this book that neither of those assumptions has yet been shown to be correct. Although they have not yet been demonstrated to be incorrect, that is a much harder thing to prove and, therefore, it is suggested here that the time has come to question them. If the assumptions are wrong that would explain why the search for entrepreneurship based on them led to much confusion and, as this book's title suggests, to more questions than answers. Also, if that is the case, then a conscious decision to abandon the assumptions would help to free research to explore different, and possibly more productive, areas.

It has not always been like this, and in the 1980s and 1990s it might have seemed that progress was being made. For instance one commentator writing in 1992 observed that in the late 1970s entrepreneurship had been a 'tangible activity, academically "flaky" and lacking in a scholarly body of knowledge' and that 'little research in entrepreneurship [went] on and consequently the literature on it remained thin'.[19] However, he reported, since then not only had there been 'a dramatic increase in the entrepreneurship literature' but also there was 'a positive movement toward a commonly accepted definition of entrepreneurship and toward the definition of the boundaries of the field of entrepreneurship'.[20] But today it seems clear that that apparent movement was an illusion, and already in 2000, when

Gibb talked about 'an explosion of research into entrepreneurship and the small and medium enterprise', he also added that 'despite the increase in academic knowledge, indeed perhaps because of it, there has been a growth of ignorance' (ignorance which he defined from *Chambers Dictionary* as 'an absence of knowledge in a particular arena that might fairly be expected to be overcome').[21] Since then, if anything, the situation has become less clear – a review of the search indicates that we have identified a wide variety of people as entrepreneurs and have applied the label 'entrepreneurship' to various things – some of which appear to be so different from each other that it is hard to see them as the same thing.

Is this like trying to fit together the different pieces of a jigsaw puzzle so that successively the picture becomes clearer? Or is the reality that we are trying to make one picture from a jumble of pieces from different puzzles – in which case the confusion will continue? So far we have largely assumed that it is the former and that entrepreneurship as we have understood it is essentially one homogeneous distinguishable condition which leads the people affected by it to become entrepreneurs (and thus to start and/or grow businesses). Therefore, we have sought more information which we expect will eventually start to clarify the picture. However, that effort has not been fruitful – instead of the emergence of clarification and a widespread agreement about entrepreneurship and its behaviours and attributes, the confusion continues and we still don't have a single commonly accepted definition of what entrepreneurship is.

As its title suggests, this book contends that the search for entrepreneurship has produced more questions than answers – but what are the implications of that? Should we consider the possibility that entrepreneurship does not exist as we have conceived it? Even if it is not completely proved, could accepting the possibility that what we think of as entrepreneurship is not all the same thing, and is not a single definable deterministic condition, free our thinking to accommodate valuable new insights?

Notes

1 R. S. Edwards and H. Townsend, *Business Enterprise: Its Growth and Organisation* (London: Macmillan, reprinted 1967).
2 Ibid., pp. 6–7.
3 A. A. Gibb, 'SME Policy, Academic Research and the Growth of Ignorance, Mythical Concepts, Myths, Assumptions, Rituals and Confusions', *International Small Business Journal*, Vol.18 No.3, 2000, pp. 2–12.
4 J. A. Katz, 'The Chronology and Intellectual Trajectory of American Entrepreneurship Education 1876–1999', *Journal of Business Venturing*, Vol.18 No.2, 2003, p. 295.
5 G. R. Plaschka, ICSB Senior Vice President, writing in the *Bulletin of the International Council for Small Business* Vol.24 No.1, Winter 1992.

6 Kauffman Foundation, *Entrepreneurship Education Comes of Age on Campus* (Kansas City: Ewing Marion Kauffman Foundation, 2013), p. 1.
7 M. Meyer, D. Libaers, B. Thijs, K. Grant, W. Glanzel and K. Debackere, *Origin and Emergence of Entrepreneurship as a Research Field* (Belgium: KU Leuven, Faculty of Economics and Business, April 2013).
8 Welsh Assembly Government, *Economic Renewal: A New Direction* (Cardiff: Welsh Assembly Government, July 2010), p. 43.
9 European Commission, *The Entrepreneurship 2020 Action Plan*, www.ec.europa. eu/growth/smes/promoting-entrepreneurship/action-plan/index_en.htm (accessed 26 December 2015).
10 Secretary of State John Kerry in 2014 quoted by D. B. Audretsch, D. F. Kuratko and A. N. Link, *Making Sense of the Elusive Paradigm of Entrepreneurship* (The University of North Carolina, Greensboro: Department of Economics Working Paper 15–04, April 2015), p. 5.
11 G20 Leaders' Communiqué, Brisbane Summit, November 2014, https://g20.org (accessed 18 January 2015).
12 C. Karlsson, *Political Entrepreneurship, Cluster Policies and Regional Growth*, CESIS Working Paper Series Paper No.407 (Sweden: The Royal Institute of Technology Centre of Excellence for Science and Innovation Studies, 2015).
13 D. L. Birch, *The Job Generation Process*, unpublished report prepared for the Economic Development Administration (Cambridge, MA: MIT Program on Neighborhood and Regional Change, 1979).
14 D. L. Birch, 'Who Creates Jobs?', *The Public Interest*, Vol.65 1981, p. 7.
15 Ibid., pp. 5–7.
16 J. Haltiwanger, R. S. Jarmin and J. Miranda, 'Who Creates Jobs? Small vs Large vs Young', in *Centre for Economic Studies Research Papers CES10–17* (Washington, DC: Centre for Economic Studies, 2010).
17 M. Henrekson, *Entrepreneurship, Innovation and Human Flourishing* (Stockholm: Research Institute of Industrial Economics, IFN Working Paper No.999, January 2014), p. 2.
18 P. Nightingale and A. Coad, *Muppets and Gazelles: Political and Methodological Biases in Entrepreneurship Research* (Brighton: University of Sussex, SPRU Working Paper SWPS 2013–13, September 2013), p. 7.
19 G. R. Plaschka, Op Cit.
20 Ibid.
21 A. A. Gibb, Op Cit.

2 A history of work (and the options for addressing life needs)

'Work is the curse of the drinking classes.'

Oscar Wilde

'Work is a necessary evil to be avoided.'

Mark Twain

Entrepreneurship, if it exists, occurs in the context of what most people think of as work – so this chapter examines the history of work as the field in which entrepreneurs have operated and in which entrepreneurship might therefore be identified. It is easy to supply humorous quotes about work, especially about work as something to be avoided, but throughout history work has been an essential and continuing part of the lives of almost everyone. Why is this – why is work such an issue and why do people want, or feel they have, to work? A quick answer is that they work in order to address their needs which, Maslow suggested, come in a hierarchy starting with basic survival needs and then rising, through safety, belonging and esteem needs, to a need for self-actualisation. Table 2.1 lists some of these possible reasons – which can be related to Maslow's hierarchy, albeit listed more or less in the reverse order.

Work can obtain results directly or indirectly. If you are hungry you can satisfy that hunger directly by working to hunt, gather or grow food – or indirectly by working to earn money with which to buy food – and the same goes for clothing or shelter. Overall most people work to obtain the resources they need for living, and there are a variety of ways in which they might do this. Some ways might appeal because they don't actually involve much work. For instance, inheriting or marrying wealth or winning the lottery may not take much effort, but these options are not available to many people. Begging or crime are the methods adopted by others, even if they are socially and/or legally discouraged – and they are still forms of work and generally require some effort. However, for most people, depending on where they live, the main possibilities have been one or more of

Table 2.1 Reasons why people might want to work

- To obtain the resources needed to survive, live and/or to raise a family.
- To feel part of a group or community.
- To earn respect and influence – to be famous and/or to have status.
- To obtain the means with which to acquire pleasure and gratification.
- To make a fortune.
- To make a contribution to society and to other people.
- To achieve success, for instance, in sport, exploration or science.
- To create art and/or to express themselves through art.

Source: Based on S. Bridge, *Rethinking Enterprise Policy* (Basingstoke: Palgrave Macmillan, 2010), p. 151.

hunter-gathering, self-sufficient agriculture, working for someone else or having a business enterprise of some sort. The evolution of those activities is therefore the subject of this chapter's history of work.

Hunter-gathering

Our ancestors may have diverged from the ancestors of today's apes many years ago, but it is clear that for most of that time they continued to feed themselves by hunting and catching wild animals and fish and finding and gathering wild plants and fruit. It also seems that during this time they lived in relatively small mobile family or tribal groups, not least because hunter-gathering generally does not support large concentrated static populations.

Compared to the pace of modern development, hunter-gatherers seem to have produced few innovations. There are some, of course, with the use of fire, the making of spears and bows and arrows for hunting and the crafting of stone tools being obvious examples, but not a lot for the many thousands of years of this stage of human existence. Either as a result of this or as a reason for it, there appears to have been very little, if any, specialisation in activity. Studies of surviving hunter-gatherer societies indicate that everything is done more or less by everyone in and for the family group – and certainly there are no such things as distinct public, private and third economic sectors. Thus the reality is that hunter-gathering was then the only available means of securing food – apart from possibly by taking it from others in occasional inter-tribal raids.

The advent of agriculture

However about 11,000 years ago an alternative to hunter-gathering started to evolve through what has been called the agricultural revolution. Humans began to produce food by domesticating wild animals and cultivating wild plants. Developing agriculture is not a quick process. It takes time to discover which animals can be domesticated and to breed more malleable or productive varieties of them, and cultivated crops often appear to be the result of a long process of selective breeding of particularly helpful mutations. Although primitive farmers often have to work for longer than hunter-gatherers, nevertheless agricultural techniques make it possible to extract more edible food from a given area of land.

Agriculture also has an advantage when it comes to surpluses. Although hunter-gatherers occasionally acquire more food than they can consume, the surplus is often hard to store and so is of little use. Agriculture, in contrast, often provides surpluses which can be stored – for instance, grain can be kept in granaries and animals can be kept alive in fields. Storable surpluses permit full-time non–food-producing specialists to operate because they can be 'paid' in something which is not immediately perishable. Thus it facilitates the establishment of tradesmen like smiths and wheelwrights as well as a ruling class supported by bureaucrats.

In this way agriculture facilitates specialists – and the development of stratified societies in which those in some levels can have the time and inclination for innovation. Necessity may be the mother of invention, but innovations also need society support for their development. Writing, for instance, may have been developed to record taxes gathered, but for its evolution beyond that it also needed a society which could support the scribes who learned and specialised in it.

Thus a consequence of the agricultural revolution was societies with denser populations and which could store food and so pay dues, taxes or wages with that stored food. This, it is suggested, assisted the emergence of societies which seem to have had a higher rate of innovation than hunter-gatherer ones, although still relatively slow by modern standards.[1] As well as the invention of writing, other key innovations from the agricultural period have included metallurgy and the wheel. And another feature of stratified societies was that the people employed to implement the governmental decisions of rulers were often working outside their family circles. However, although there began to be some non-family employment like this, many people still worked for and/or in family units.

Social evolution

The agricultural revolution may have created the conditions which could support invention and innovation by some people. One feature of agricultural societies is that they are usually hierarchical with a relatively small class of rulers and some specialists supported by the rest – and it was some among those who were thus freed from the day-to-day drudgery of productive work who may have been the main innovators. For instance, as suggested earlier, writing may have originated in systems used by early bureaucrats to record transactions, such as the payment of taxes or tributes – and was then developed by those with the time and inclination and in scripts which were influenced by the materials available such as simple symbols for clay tablets or pictograms for ink and papyrus.[2]

Box 2.1   The advent of money

A development in human affairs with clear links to the economic world was the introduction of money. It used to be assumed, possibly because it seemed so logical, that money was invented to replace direct barter as a way of exchanging goods and/or services. Before money was invented it was thought that people were only able to exchange one good or service for another, and so trade was restricted when the person who wanted what you were offering did not have anything that you wanted in exchange. Therefore, it was supposed, to avoid the necessity for complicated barter systems involving three or more parties to each transaction, certain goods, such as sugar in the West Indies, tobacco in Virginia and dried cod in Newfoundland,[3] were used as agreed media of exchange because everyone recognised that they had a value and would thus accept them as payment because they knew others would in turn accept them in exchange for what they were offering. In time these consumable media of exchange were replaced by things such as precious metals, often in the form of minted coins, and then coins of other metals and eventually paper notes, as these became accepted as more practical substitutes for the earlier, more perishable media of exchange.

However, the problem with this assumption is that it appears not to be true. No one has found an actual example of even a primitive society which uses barter in the form envisaged in this supposition, and it is clear that relatively complex societies, such as those portrayed in the *Iliad* and the *Odyssey*, functioned without money. What records there are indicate that before money people exchanged goods or services, not for a medium of exchange, but for credit – and money started as a way of quantifying the extent of someone's credit.[4] After all many coins have little intrinsic value, and even those of precious metal have had nominal values greater than that of their metal content, so that value of a coin is the amount of credit in the system that its possession signifies. However, when money was represented by portable things like coins, then people did begin to use it directly to make purchases.

Ancient Greece provides a good case study for the introduction of money, both because relatively good descriptions of that period have survived and because it is clear that it developed a commercial economy significantly later than some of its neighbours. The Homeric warriors appeared to shun trade and, as indicated earlier, did not deal in money. They did, however, deal in possessions, prizes, loot and slaves, and their worth or honour could be shown by the extent of their treasure and followers. When coins were introduced, they were used for the payment of fines, for payments to 'government' such as taxes – and for paying soldiers. By about 600 BCE most Greek city-states seem to have had a coinage and, by the next century, an *agora* which served as a place for public debate and as a marketplace. However, it is also clear that those at the top of Greek society saw money almost as the embodiment of corruption, believing that a man of honour should be able to raise everything he wanted from his estates (which were tended by his slaves) and thus have no need to handle cash at all.[5]

Therefore some societies appear to have developed a form of exchange for high-class social transactions, such as ransoms and payments to temples, and a lower-class one for commercial exchange. In these cases it seems that it was the initially lower-class usage that survived and developed and, despite the disdain of people like the Greek ruling classes, money clearly helped in the world of work and commercial exchange and greatly facilitated the buying and selling of goods and services. It might not have been invented to facilitate these transactions, but it did make them easier.

Clearly it was the rulers and the ruling classes for whom tributes or taxes were collected (whether in kind or cash) and, whether they ruled by permission or fear, those rulers liked their lifestyle and sought to perpetuate it by devising ways of extracting from the producing classes the outputs needed to support or enhance the rulers' way of life. And, as well as extracting taxes and/or tributes, they directly harnessed the efforts of some productive workers through slavery.

Classical Rome was one example of a society with a ruling class which lived by extractive means. It conquered an empire from which it extracted tribute and throughout the empire itself slavery was widespread. However, in Western Europe another extractive institution evolved which started to make slavery largely redundant and that was feudalism. Feudalism was a feature of some agricultural societies in which each level of society owed an obligation to the higher level. At the lowest level were the serfs, who were the majority of the population and who typically farmed for themselves in communal fields but were also obliged to work part of the time for their lords. Thus the serfs had little incentive to innovate and work better because any improvement largely benefitted others, and the lords also had little incentive to change because the system already worked to their benefit and, in any case, change was unsettling and therefore threatening.

At least in parts of Western Europe it seems it was the advent of the plague which led to the end of feudalism because the high death rate increased the bargaining power of the surviving labourers. In places like England, the ending of feudalism and the replacement of extractive systems by inclusive ones (see Chapter 8) allowed a lot more people a freer choice in how they could earn the resources they needed. Of course, their choice was limited by the opportunities available, but, because others could not unfairly limit this, they could be reasonably sure of being able to keep the results of their industry. They were thus freer to explore the possibilities they saw, and there was more incentive to innovate and try new methods – and this, it is suggested, was one of the factors which may have facilitated the Industrial Revolution.

Another significant development in Europe was science. In the 11th century Europe was technically backward compared to both China and the Islamic empire, but by the 18th century, Europe was clearly in the lead. Further, Lipsey et al. argue, within Europe, England was ahead because it had Newtonian-led 'mechanical' science which was the sort of science needed to support and facilitate technological developments. The development of science itself was facilitated by the evolution of universities which provided the 'institutional memory' needed to record, preserve and promulgate such learning.[6] And, as Acemoglu and Robinson[7] point out, technology and education are two of the key 'engines' of prosperity which are facilitated and/or encouraged by inclusive economic institutions.

Industrial development

Science played a key part in the Industrial Revolution. The development of textile machines might have been due more to the tinkering of intelligent craftsmen than the lessons of science, but the move of such work from the home into factories was necessary if water and later steam power was to be harnessed to the machines – and harnessing steam power depended on the application of the relevant science and on investment – and inclusive institutions were needed to encourage people to invest the time and resources needed. England also had potential investors encouraged by inclusive institutions and science supported by universities, and it was in England that the Industrial Revolution started and grew – and work in England started to change as a result (see also Chapter 8).

By the time that the Industrial Revolution began, another aspect of economic organisation was also becoming clear – the emergence of different economic sectors. In hunter-gatherer societies everyone works for the family group and so did most people in early agricultural societies, whether that was in direct food production or in small specialist enterprises such as smiths and leather workers. However, once the effects of agriculture began to be realised in hierarchical structures, some people were employed outside their families to serve the needs and implement the wishes of the rulers which, as indicated earlier, could be said to be the start of public-sector employment.

It was high-risk but potentially high-return explorations of people like Columbus which highlighted the need for a way of creating a recognised non-family commercial enterprise and in particular for a form of organisation which facilitated risk sharing by investors. This led to the limited liability company which reduced the personal risk involved in owning a business. Adam Smith is said to have opposed limited liability companies because he thought that they would lead to owners being less vigilant in monitoring their managers and, until the middle of the 19th century, in England such companies needed a royal charter. Nevertheless it has been said that it was their evolution which made modern capitalism possible.[8] In England the East India Company was an early example of a business clearly established with a separate legal identity, as it derived its powers from a royal charter of 1600, and a parallel example from the Netherlands is the formation of the Vereenigde Nederlandsche Geoctroyeerde Oostindische Compaagnie (United Dutch Chartered East India Company) in 1602.[9] Such initiatives accompanied and assisted the emergence of a merchant class whose business was in trade rather than in farming or artisanal production.

Fordism – and the growth of big businesses

A key feature of the Industrial Revolution was specialist machinery which greatly increased the potential output per employee (labour productivity) and meant that goods could be produced at relatively low unit costs. However that was generally only possible if the machines were located in factories to which the labourers would come to work at set times, instead of 'putting out' work which they did at home as and when they could. These large plants could capture market share because they could produce a lot and sell it cheaply – but they also needed that market share because they needed to sell a lot to recoup the cost of that machinery and the cost of the plant needed to supply power for it. This is the effect of economies of scale, and it started a trend towards larger plants with lower unit costs. It was also accompanied by horizontal and vertical integration to co-locate as many parts of the overall process as possible in order to be able to control and co-ordinate them. A significant exponent of this, after whom the process has been named, was Henry Ford with his production lines.

By the middle of the 20th century, the future seemed to be Fordism, with its large integrated production plants and its economies of scale. While there were still a lot of small businesses, often they were not seen as being in any significant way distinct from bigger businesses. As noted in Chapter 1, the author still has the first business textbook he was advised to read which was initially published in 1958[10] and which does not consider small businesses as worthy of separate consideration.

When small businesses did receive recognition at this time, it was generally because they were thought to be in decline and were being seen almost as an endangered species. For example, in the United States the Small Business Administration (SBA) was established in 1953 to help preserve the small business sector there, and in the UK the Committee of Inquiry on Small Firms was set up in 1969 under the chairmanship of JE Bolton (the Bolton Committee) to consider the role of small firms in a modern economy. Therefore, it can be said that in both administrations at that time, where small businesses were recognised as a relevant category meriting official concern, any resultant policy was largely preservationist, not expansionist.[11] Therefore, because of developments such as Fordism and the industrial effort stimulated by the Second World War and the stable levels of relatively full employment that followed that conflict, it seemed that most people in the more developed countries could, if they acquired an appropriate skill, expect to have a job for life mainly as an employee of some form of large enterprise.

Employment and self-employment

The period from 1840 to 1990 has been referred to by one observer as the 'age of the job' because it was only after 1840 that people started to have fixed hours of work and to be paid salaries.[12] However, according to Urwin,[13] it was not until the start of 20th century that a clear distinction between 'employees' and the 'self-employed' emerged. Before that, he suggests, although employers may have held the balance of power in the years before widespread unionisation, workers were not systematically held to fixed periods of notice, and the relationship between business owners and workers was more or less the same as that which had prevailed for itinerant workers since antiquity. However, industrialised employers needed to exercise greater control over large numbers of workers – for instance, when organising shift-working by employees skilled in the operation of expensive machinery. The employers therefore wanted enforceable contracts of employment, and the workers responded in return by organising to demand things like holiday and sick pay. Thus, largely through case law, the distinction emerged between those who were employed long term under a *contract of service* and those who were instead self-employed and worked on short-term *contracts for services*.

Box 2.2   Freelance work

One area of employment in which an early form of contract employment emerged was warfare. Although many soldiers were recruited by their rulers, either voluntarily or compulsorily, to fight for their side, other soldiers were mercenaries who fought for whoever paid them. Among the mercenaries who found ready employment in the 16th and 17th centuries were lancers (or pikemen). A lance is a spear-like weapon which was used by cavalry and then, in a longer form also known as a pike, by infantry as a weapon against cavalry. So successful was this application that lances and/or pikes were used in almost every European army, and the men who knew how to wield them could, if they wished, become sought-after mercenaries. Those mercenaries were not tied just to one cause but were free to use their lances for whoever was prepared to pay for them. Thus, in 1820 in his novel *Ivanhoe*, Sir Walter Scott used the term 'free lance' to describe a mercenary warrior of the medieval period – a soldier who fought not exclusively for just one cause, but who could be hired by any side for an agreed period:

> I offered Richard the service of my Free Lances, and he refused them. (But) . . . thanks to the bustling times, a man of action will always find employment.[14]

Therefore whether workers became employees or self-employed depended to a considerable extent on the trade they had chosen, or been selected, to follow. Those working in industry and with skills which were required every day largely became employees, but others with skills which were only needed occasionally and/or for relatively short periods often remained self-employed. So those people trained as welders or machinists were likely to be employed, whereas hairdressers and window cleaners had trades in which many people were and are self-employed.

But this category of self-employment covers many eventualities. Bögenhold et al. comment that 'differences between positions within self-employment can be higher than differences between individual self-employed people and employees'.[15] Self-employment includes people who work as freelancers in fields such as journalism and translation, often because they do not want to be tied to a permanent full-time job, and it also includes many artists. Some of those who work on a freelance basis might consider themselves to be professionals, a category which includes people like architects, doctors and lawyers. Bögenhold et al. refer to a long-lasting debate on the question of whether professionals act differently to 'regular' businessmen. Classically, they suggest businessmen are seen as having an 'egoistic' motivation, 'pursuing [their] self-interest regardless of the interests of others', whereas liberal professionals 'altruistically serve the interests of others regardless of their own'.[16] Although some professionals might form partnerships rather than working on their own, nevertheless, as Bögenhold et al. suggest, they can be regarded as self-employed, albeit in a sub-set of the self-employment spectrum.

The third wave

As explained earlier, by the 1950s and after the upsets of the 1930s and the Second World War, big businesses with their economies of scale seemed to be the future and small businesses largely a diminishing survival from the past. For about 30 years after the war many countries had experienced relatively low and relatively static levels of unemployment, but in the 1970s there was a rise in unemployment which did not seem to respond to the then-accepted economic remedies. Therefore the release in 1979 of Birch's findings that, in the United States, it was small businesses, not big ones, which were the net creators of jobs[17] led to a lot of re-thinking. Not everyone agreed with Birch, and his conclusions have at various times been challenged – but the message that small businesses are economically important has survived.

Actually they had not been completely ignored. Penrose had studied the growth of firms which led her to realise that firms did not in reality grow as theory supposed. She explored this in her second book, *The Theory of the Growth of the Firm*,[18] in which, among other issues, she reflected on the changes of management and administration needed as a firm grew in size. Thus she described how small firms are structured and behave very differently from big ones. As firms grow larger, she said, it is 'likely that their organisation will become so different that we must look on them differently;

we cannot define a caterpillar and then use the same definition for a butterfly'.[19] She also considered the comparative advantages of small and large firms concluding, for instance, that larger firms did not always have an advantage. The Bolton Report (from the Bolton Committee – see earlier) also emphasised the importance of small businesses. It came out in 1971 and emphasised that the small firm sector was 'of substantial importance to the UK economy' and 'the contribution of small businessmen to the vitality of society is inestimable'.[20]

In his book *The Third Wave*,[21] originally published in 1980, Toffler suggested that significant waves of change in human development had followed the agricultural and industrial revolutions. The first wave, triggered by agriculture, had by then reached all but a very few remaining tribal societies, and the second wave, with its accompanying industrialisation, had reached many people but was still not entirely spent. Nevertheless, he suggested, they were already being succeeded by a third wave. What Toffler thought third wave was seems, with an element of retrospect, to be less clear. He mentioned Silicon Valley and solid-state physics as well as electronics and computers, in addition to the space industry and exploring the seas' depths, and biology and genetics – and it now seems that it was the first four of those which have had the greatest impact.

Others also observed a change and noted that in developed countries, there has been a shift from manufacturing to services.[22] Just as the Industrial Revolution had led to a move of employment away from the land, so, too, was the third wave being accompanied by a move of employment away from manufacturing. And it is also relevant that services can be less dependent on economies of scale and therefore more likely to be delivered by small businesses. So, as in many things, no change is final and, as agriculture replaced hunter-gathering as the main economic activity, so it was in turn replaced in many countries by manufacturing which, in some economies, is itself being superseded by services – leaving the question open of what will eventually take over from them.

However, a number of points need to be made about these moves. The move of employment away from the land did not mean less food production. Often more food was produced by much more efficient and mechanised working but using less labour. Nevertheless countries like England, with limited space and with rapidly rising populations, also needed to import more food and therefore, in effect, to export some food production. And the labour that moved from the land did not all move into industry, but, as Brown and Julius report, often into the service sector. Today manufacture is not the distinctive prerogative of developed countries. Manufacturers who want to compete on cost are shifting manufacturing to developing countries, and those who want to compete on high value added will have to raise their intensive customisation and associated services – and both these routes will hasten an employment shift to services. Therefore, they suggest, manufacturing should now no longer be seen as special and that, overall, momentum has been 'building for a global economic transformation'.[23]

According to Audretsch et al. a major shift in the organisation of developed economies has indeed been taking place – from 'managed' economies, where economic performance is positively related to 'firm size, scale economics and routinized production', to 'entrepreneurial' economies where performance 'is related to distributed innovation and the emergence and growth of innovative ventures'.[24] The fundamental catalyst for this, they observe, has been technological change and, in particular, the emergence of information and communication technologies (ICT), but, they suggest, other factors have been involved also, including globalisation, the demise of the communist system and rising levels of prosperity.

ICT, they suggest, has significantly reduced the marginal cost of communication, so small firms can compete on even terms. It has also been accompanied by an increased reliance, not on organisation, but on knowledge and innovation where small firms can have a distinct advantage. With the ease, speed and global availability of electronic communication, key suppliers no longer need to be on the same site, and once again separate small organisations can often be competitive due to specialisation, flexibility and lower overheads.

Some of the trend towards contract work and away from employment might be because it is easier to find work that way rather than because it is preferred. For instance in 2014 it was reported that in Massachusetts increasing numbers of people, tired of waiting for suitable job opportunities, were using on-line referral sites to look for project work as independent contractors.[25]

Therefore, although the third wave and associated entrepreneurial economies may still be relatively new and their full nature and lasting impact therefore hard to assess, nevertheless it does seem that, in terms of people's work options, they will lead to more change, fewer jobs for life, more opportunities for innovation and small enterprises and more dependence on thinking and knowledge rather than on dexterity and manual skills.

Notes

1 J. Diamond, *Guns, Germs and Steel* (London: Vintage, 1998).
2 R. G. Lipsey, K. I. Carlaw and C. T. Bekar, *Economic Transformations: General Purpose Technologies and Long Term Economic Growth* (Oxford: Oxford University Press, 2005), pp. 144–150.
3 F. Martin, *Money: The Unauthorised Biography* (London: Vintage, 2014), back cover.

4 D. Graeber, *Debt: The First 5,000 Years* (London: Melville House, 2014).
5 Ibid., pp. 186–187.
6 R. G. Lipsey et al., Op Cit, p. 260.
7 D. Acemoglu and J. A. Robinson, *Why Nations Fail: The Origins of Power, Prosperity and Poverty* (London: Profile Books, 2013), p. 77.
8 J.-H. Chang, *23 Things They Don't Tell You about Capitalism* (London: Penguin, 2011), p. 12.
9 N. Ferguson, *The Ascent of Money* (London: Penguin Books, 2009), p. 128.
10 R. S. Edwards and H. Townsend, *Business Enterprise: Its Growth and Organisation* (London: Macmillan, 1967).
11 S. Bridge and K. O'Neill, *Understanding Enterprise, Entrepreneurship and Small Business* (Basingstoke: Palgrave Macmillan, 2013), pp. 16–18.
12 W. Bridges, 'Redefining Work', *RSA Journal*, Vol.1 No.4, 1998, p. 50.
13 P. Urwin, *Self-Employment, Small Firms and Enterprise* (London: Institute of Economic Affairs in association with Profile Books Ltd., 2011).
14 Sir Walter Scott, *Ivanhoe* (first published 1819) (London: Guild Publishing, 1982), p. 317.
15 D. Bögenhold, J. Heinonen and E. Akola, *Entrepreneurship and Independent Professionals: Why Do Professionals Not Meet with Stereotypes of Entrepreneurship* (Alpen-Adria-Universität, Austria: Deportment of Sociology, IfS Discussion Paper, April, 2013), p. 9.
16 D. Bögenhold, et al., Op Cit, p. 7.
17 D. L. Birch, *The Job Generation Process*, unpublished report prepared for the Economic Development Administration (Cambridge, MA: MIT Program on Neighborhood and Regional Change, 1979).
18 E. T. Penrose, *The Theory of the Growth of the Firm* (New York: John Wiley and Sons, 1959 and Oxford: Basil Blackwell, 1959).
19 Ibid., p. 19.
20 J. E. Bolton (Chairman), *Report of the Committee of Inquiry on Small Firms* (London: HMSO, 1971), p. 344.
21 A. Toffler, *The Third Wave* (London: Collins, 1980).
22 R. Brown and D. Julius, 'Is manufacturing still special in the new world order?', in J. Drew (ed), *Readings in International Enterprise* (London: Routledge, 1995), pp. 275–285.
23 Ibid., p. 275.
24 D. B. Audretsch, A. R. Thurik and E. Stam, *Unraveling the Shift to the Entrepreneurial Economy* (Zoetermeer, Netherlands: EIM, 2011).
25 New Jobs for Massachusetts, *Telegram and Gazette*, 31 January 2014, www.newmassjobs.com.

3 Observations of entrepreneurs – and entrepreneurship

Chapter 2 provides an outline history of how the world of work has evolved and of the various ways in which people have sought to secure the resources they need to live and/or to self-actualise. Intentionally that outline does not refer to entrepreneurs or entrepreneurship because that is what this chapter examines. It seeks to indicate where, in the different forms and contexts of work described in Chapter 2, different observers claim to have identified entrepreneurs or supposed that entrepreneurship might exist. In effect it seeks to add entrepreneurship as an overlay to the historical map indicated in the previous chapter, and it also indicates the sort of activity which was thus identified as entrepreneurship.

Inevitably these are mostly recent observations – not because entrepreneurship is thought to be a new phenomenon but because the concept of entrepreneurship has only relatively recently been articulated, and it is only in the last 30 to 40 years that it has been thoroughly explored.

Early observations of entrepreneurs

> 'That most noble centoure Publius Decius so hardie an entreprennoure in the bataile.'
>
> Quote from 1475[1]

The term *entrepreneur* is a French word which, according to Filion, first appeared in 1253,[2] and the *Oxford English Dictionary* records the use of the word 'entreprennoure' in English in 1475 – although not in an economic context (see the earlier quote). Its introduction to the vocabulary of economics is generally attributed to Richard Cantillon, an Irishman who went to live in France in about 1690 where he was an entrepreneur and a banker, earning money from stock market trading. He is reputed to have died in London in 1734, although it has been suggested that this might not have been the case. Nevertheless he recorded his observations on the economic system of his day in his *Essai sur la nature du commerce en général*[3] although it was not published until 1755.

In his *Essai*, Cantillon used the word 'entrepreneur' to describe people who were an important component in the economic system. According to him there were three main sorts of economic actors: there were the landlords who owned the land; there were the labourers who worked, often for the landowners, for a wage; and there were the entrepreneurs. Both the land-owners and the labourers, Cantillon suggested, had incomes which were agreed to in advance, whether from renting out their land or hiring out their labour. In contrast the entrepreneurs had fixed costs, such as the rent for the land they used or the wages of the people they employed, but uncertain income because it depended on factors beyond their control. Thus a farmer promised to pay to the landowner a fixed sum for the land which he farmed and used to grow crops, but how much he grew and the price for which he could sell those crops would be determined by factors such as the weather and the level of demand at the time the crops were ready to be sold. Because these variables cannot be foreseen in advance, the farmer 'consequently conducts the enterprise of his farm at an uncertainty'.[4] Therefore Cantillon was using the word *entrepreneur* as a label for what he actually saw, rather than for something he expected or wanted to see.

Cantillon might thus be said to have been describing the concept now labelled in English as 'entrepreneurship'. However his *Essai* was published in French, although there has been some speculation that it might have been a translation from a lost English original.[5] Although the French verb 'entre-prendre' could be translated as 'to take between', it may be of interest that when the *Essai* was translated into English by Higgs in about 1930 he used the English word 'undertaker' as the nearest English equivalent of '*entre-preneur*'. This suggests that, even though Cantillon in the 18th century is credited as being the source of our use of the word, around 200 years later it was still not in common use in England.

Before Cantillon

Although Cantillon, in first using the word entrepreneur in this way, was writing in the early 18th century, the term has subsequently been applied to earlier periods. In accordance with Cantillon's use of the word the mer-chants who traded along the silk route, buying in one place in the hope, but not the certainty, of being able to sell for a profit in another, were entrepre-neurs.[6] And in the sense of entrepreneurs being enterprising people, Baumol has suggested that they have been present in all societies – although how they act at any given time has depended on their society's reward structures (see Box 3.1).

Box 3.1   A historical view of entrepreneurs

Baumol has commented on the presence of entrepreneurs in times and places such as ancient Rome, medieval China and middle-age Europe – but he uses an interpretation of entrepreneurs as 'persons who are ingenious and creative in finding ways that add to their own wealth, power, and prestige'[7] which can be in any field, not just in business.

His hypothesis is that:

> while the total supply of entrepreneurs varies among societies, the productive contribution of the society's entrepreneurial activities varies much more because of their allocation between productive . . . and largely unproductive activities . . . [and that] this allocation is heavily influenced by the relative payoffs society offers to such activities.[8]

For him entrepreneurs have always been with us but the ways in which an entrepreneurial person's efforts can be allocated do not all follow the constructive script conventionally attributed to such a person. For instance in ancient Rome, he suggests, persons of honourable status had no reservations about the desirability of wealth or its pursuit – so long as it did not involve participation in manufacture or commerce. For those who had or sought prestige, there were three primary and acceptable ways to make money: landholding, usury and political payments – but being entrepreneurial in those areas was not productive. It was possible for entrepreneurs to make money in commerce and industry, but those who did that could not also have prestige.

In medieval China, Baumol reports, the most substantial rewards in both prestige and wealth were reserved for those who climbed the ladder of the imperial bureaucracy – which also meant an unproductive application of any entrepreneurial ability, not least because any wealth was often obtained through corruption and the state clamped down on private enterprise. Things were, if anything, worse in early middle-age Europe where wealth was often sought through warfare and where, in places like England, the institution of primogeniture meant that only the first-born sons inherited wealth, and warfare was almost the only acceptable outlet for the enterprise of second and subsequent sons of nobles. Although warfare may have led to innovations, such as the introduction of the stirrup for cavalry and gunpowder for artillery, it was nevertheless a very destructive way to use entrepreneurial ability.[9]

Baumol uses the term 'entrepreneurship' for what he is describing. He also highlights a notion held by some 'that our productivity problems reside in "the spirit of entrepreneurship" that waxes and wanes for unexplained reasons' – but, he adds, this 'is a council of despair, for it gives no guidance on how to reawaken that spirit once it has lagged'.[10]

Innovation, creative destruction and economic growth

Cantillon was working in France at the start of the 18th century, and it was in France also about a century after that that one of the next main contributions to thinking about entrepreneurs came from Jean-Baptiste Say. He is probably best known for Say's Law which has been variously stated in ways such as 'supply creates its own demand' and 'if you build it, they will come'. However, although he discussed and promulgated this thinking, it seems he did not originate it. Say's principal work, *Traité d'économie politique ou simple exposition de la manière dont se forment, se distribuent et se composent les richesses*, was published in 1803, and he is credited with identifying the element of innovation as a key characteristic of entrepreneurs: it is about doing something new, whether that is a new product, or service, or a new process. Thus, for Say, there was a distinction between the entrepreneur who did something new and the capitalist who may have been at risk in funding those efforts.

Living another hundred or so years after Say was Joseph Schumpeter who was born in 1883 in Austria-Hungary, studied and worked in Vienna and then, after a spell in a German university, went to the United States. Among his contributions was the identification of creative destruction as a key outcome from the entrepreneurial process – and the main mechanism for economic development. Schumpeter's most popular book in English is probably *Capitalism, Socialism and Democracy* which was first published in 1942. In it he repeated Say's emphasis on innovation but extended it to other forms of newness and pointed out that something new often replaces something old and thus 'creatively' destroys the old thing and the processes associated with it.

Schumpeter's early contributions were written in German, and he coined the word '*Unternehmergeist*' ('entrepreneur-spirit') which has been translated into English as 'entrepreneurship'. His interpretation of this concept based on innovation is indicated in the following passage:

[It] covers the following five cases: (1) the introduction of a new good – that is one with which consumers are not yet familiar – or of a new quality of a good. (2) The introduction of a new method of production, that is one not yet tested by experience in the branch of manufacture concerned, which need by no means be founded upon a discovery scientifically new, and can also exist in a new way of handling a commodity commercially. (3) The opening of a new market, that is a market into which the particular branch of manufacture of the country in question has not previously entered, whether or not this market has existed before. (4) The conquest of a new source of supply of raw materials or half-manufactured goods, again irrespective of whether this source already exists or whether it has first to be created. (5) The carrying out of the new organization of any industry, like the creation of a monopoly position (for example through trustification) or the breaking up of a monopoly position.[11]

Schumpeter was writing after the effects of the Industrial Revolution had become apparent and had spread to many countries. This process of creative destruction through innovation was clear in the Industrial Revolution and is an inevitable, and even essential, part of evolution, even in nature. There had been many instances of relatively sudden and quite localised growth in history, such as the Renaissance in Italy, but often the growth they produced was more broadly cultural than narrowly economic. A key outcome from the Industrial Revolution, however, was economic growth, but that growth was not uniform and all countries to which the methods of the revolution spread did not achieve the same levels of growth. McClelland, as a psychologist, decided to investigate why different countries at different times achieved different levels of economic growth and produced the hypothesis that when people have higher levels of a need for achievement, which he referred to as *n* Achievement, this is associated with higher levels of economic growth. The link for this, he suggested, was that societies which have higher levels of *n* Achievement produce more energetic entrepreneurs, who, in turn, produce more economic development.[12] Thus, although he was neither an economist nor primarily focussing on entrepreneurs, McClelland clearly assumed that they were a key factor in economic growth.

Introducing the word 'entrepreneurship'

The word which, in the 18th century, Cantillon introduced from the French, was 'entrepreneur'. At that time the most commonly used English equivalents were 'adventurer', 'projector' and 'undertaker'.[13] Eventually, however, English speakers adopted the word 'entrepreneur' and then, at some stage, added the suffix 'ship' to refer to a concept associated with being an entrepreneur. This appears to have happened in the late 1920s or early 1930s, and the first source the *Oxford English Dictionary* indicates for 'entrepreneurship' is the 1934 edition of *Webster's New International Dictionary of the English Language*. The early adoption of entrepreneurship into the field of academic discourse is indicated, for instance, in a paper by Arthur Cole of Harvard University entitled 'Entrepreneurship as an Area of Research' and published in 1942.[14] Although Cole did not attempt to define entrepreneurship in the paper, he suggested that it had been a significant feature in American economic history and could be seen as a fifth factor in distribution after rent, wages, interest and profits. It was five years later in 1947, also in Harvard, that the first entrepreneurship course in the United States was said to have been delivered.[15]

Since then, as well as speaking about entrepreneurs, other commentators have used the term entrepreneurship. In retrospect it seems that the word was invented to refer to a loosely conceived concept and that it was then taken up as a useful term – for instance, when referring to the contribution of entrepreneurs to economic vitality.

Government interest in small businesses

One use of the term entrepreneurship is in government economic thinking and policy. As indicated in Chapter 2 one of the outcomes of the Industrial Revolution was Fordism, and evidence of its side effects might be seen in a reduction in the level of self-employment and a decline in numbers and economic importance of small businesses. Therefore, as indicated in Chapter 1, a significant contribution to a revival of interest in small businesses, and the processes which created them, was Birch's revelation in 1979 that at that time it was small businesses, not big ones, which were the net creators of jobs. Because unemployment was then rising in many countries, the governments of those countries looked on small businesses as a source of employment and therefore wanted more of them. Apparently in the belief that it was entrepreneurs who created small businesses and that it was entrepreneurship which produced entrepreneurs, governments wanted more entrepreneurship. Sometimes this was referred to as 'enterprise' but, whatever label was used, governments made budgets available to study, encourage and support it. Essentially, in such circles, entrepreneurship had been equated with job creation and became associated particularly with small businesses. Entrepreneurship has therefore been sought as the supposed means to an end, not as an end itself – although this distinction may sometimes be overlooked.

The influence of an economic focus

A refinement of the small-businesses-create-jobs assumption was a belief that some small businesses create more jobs than others. Birch had identified what he called 'gazelles': the small proportion of small firms that grow significantly and account for most of the growth in the sector. David Storey in 1994 asserted that 'out of every 100 [new] small firms, the fastest growing four firms will create 50 per cent of the jobs in the group over a decade'.[16] Others have found similar pictures and, for instance, in the UK in 2009 NESTA produced a report which claimed that '6 per cent of UK businesses with the highest growth rates generated half of the new jobs created by existing businesses between 2002 and 2008'.[17]

The NESTA report has been criticised, for instance by Urwin, who notes that it only includes businesses with at least ten employees at the start of the analysis period and which exhibit consistently high growth rates over three years,[18] and by Botham and Bridge, who ask if firms which grow by merger or acquisitions were included among the apparently growing businesses because those activities can actually lead to net job destruction.[19] Nevertheless policy makers have sought to focus support on the 'gazelles' on the assumption that that is where it will be most effective, and some have gone further and sought to focus on just those high-growth businesses which are high-tech and/or exporting, presumably on the basis that they are likely to deliver the highest returns in added value and export earnings.

Therefore, with this objective in mind, and presuming that it is entrepreneurship which leads to business creation, some have even tried to limit their definition of entrepreneurship only to the context of such businesses. For instance, Invest Northern Ireland, in its corporate plan for 2008–2011, declared that its Accelerating Entrepreneurship Strategy 'will increasingly emphasise the acceleration of high-potential existing and start-up companies . . . (to) provide the supply line for future exports based on new product and process innovation',[20] and a Danish entrepreneurship initiative of 2006 which was designed to help the Danish government achieve its goal that 'by 2015 Denmark (would be) among the countries with the highest start up rates of high-growth enterprises',[21] defined entrepreneurship specifically as 'the entry and creation of high-growth firms'.[22] Thus, for them, entrepreneurship was to be limited to high-tech and/or high-growth business creation.

Wider definitions

However, whereas some government agencies have thus in effect been advocating narrower definitions of entrepreneurship, others have interpreted it more widely – in a way that is similar to Baumol's view and to what others have referred to as enterprise (see Box 3.1). Examples include:

- A Scottish Enterprise paper on Enterprise and Economic Growth which states that 'entrepreneurial and enterprising behaviour is not confined to the creation of new businesses . . . and can also be found in organisations of all sizes in both private and public sectors'.[23]

- The Northern Ireland government's Entrepreneurship and Education Action Plan, published in 2003, which indicated that, for the purposes of the Action Plan, entrepreneurship was considered to be 'the ability of an individual, possessing a range of essential skills and attributes, to make a unique, innovative and creative contribution in the world of work, whether in employment or self-employment'.[24]

Box 3.2   Enterprise or entrepreneurship?

At one time it seems that many perceived a difference in meaning between the words 'entrepreneurship' and 'enterprise', with entrepreneurship being about business and business creation and enterprise having a wider meaning of the application of a set of attributes in many situations, including but not limited to, business. Therefore, in the 1980s, it seemed that governments talked about enterprise and, for instance, in the UK in 1988 the Department of Trade and Industry (DTI) launched its Enterprise Initiative in support of the view that '[w]e must have an enterprise culture, not a dependency culture'.[25]

Since then, however, such pronouncements have increasingly talked about entrepreneurship. For instance the Scottish government, in its Economic Strategy published in 2015, calls for a new spirit of entrepreneurship across the country.[26]

As a result of this trend in practice little or no distinction is made between the words enterprise and entrepreneurship, and they are treated more or less as one concept. Indeed, as a number of commentators have pointed out, today the words are often used interchangeably.[27,28]

Academic contributions – and confusion

Government interest in encouraging employment growth in small businesses led to government budgets being available, not just for small business support, but also for exploring and developing the entrepreneurship (or enterprise – see Box 3.2) that was thought to be the source of small businesses. Naturally the academic community responded to that opportunity with programmes both to research and teach entrepreneurship (and/or enterprise).

Academics had been investigating entrepreneurship before Birch, but the reaction to his findings nevertheless gave such studies an added impetus.

Schumpeter (see earlier) had made his contribution from academia, and there have been many others. One is Israel Kirzner, an English-born American economist of the Austrian School who emphasised the importance of the entrepreneur for business judgement and economic growth. Although the academic community has not had a standard approach to entrepreneurship, it has generally been assumed that it is a sub-set of business and, for instance, consistent with Kirzner, it has been asserted that 'one of the major objectives of entrepreneurship education is to provide students with the necessary skills to design, create, launch and effectively manage a business'.[29] Therefore academia has often assigned the study of entrepreneurship to business schools or departments – and many of the statements about and definitions advanced for entrepreneurship clearly place it in such a context. For instance:

> There are presently two general approaches to defining entrepreneurship. One is broadly identified with innovation and Joseph Schumpeter and the other with business creation and Israel Kirzner. The two are not mutually exclusive yet there has been a shift towards the business creation view in recent years.[30]
>
> Entrepreneurship, rigorously defined, refers to the creation of a new economic entity centred on a novel product or service or, at the very least, one which differs significantly from products or services offered elsewhere in the market.[31]
>
> Entrepreneurship is an activity that involves the discovery, evaluation and exploitation of opportunities to introduce new goods and services, ways of organising, markets, processes and raw materials through organising efforts that previously had not existed.[32]

Nevertheless others have taken a wider view. For instance:

> Entrepreneurship is the ability to create and build something from practically nothing. It is initiating, doing, achieving and building . . . rather than just watching, analysing and describing. . . . it is the knack of sensing an opportunity where other see chaos, contradiction and confusion.[33]
>
> Entrepreneurship relates to ways in which people, in all kinds of organisations behave in order to cope with and take advantage of uncertainty and complexity and how in turn this becomes embodied in: ways of doing things; ways of seeing things; ways of feeling things; ways of communicating things; and ways of learning things.[34]
>
> Entrepreneurship is the pursuit of opportunity beyond the resources currently controlled.
>
> (The Harvard Business School definition attributed to Howard Stevenson[35])

Although there are clear views about the objectives of entrepreneurship (or enterprise) education, they are not all the same, and in this field also there are different interpretations. For instance, in 1993 Gibb characterised enterprise education as being either 'about' or 'for' entrepreneurship,[36] and later Hannon added 'through' entrepreneurship as a third category.[37] The 'about', 'for' and 'through' distinctions are, in effect, those used by Hytti and Kuopusjärvi[38] who, from a perspective of evaluating entrepreneurship education, suggested that there are three different roles which they had found might be assigned to such programmes depending on what aim was being pursued. These roles might be summarised as:

- To learn to understand entrepreneurship,
- To learn to become entrepreneurial (an approach consistent with a wider interpretation of entrepreneurship)
- To learn to become an entrepreneur (generally interpreted as learning how to start a business – which assumed a relatively narrow interpretation of entrepreneurship).

There is a clear distinction in the assumed meaning of entrepreneurship between the second and third of these aims, with the third focusing more narrowly on business creation, whereas the second is about the development of enterprise abilities with a potentially wider range of applications – and it is the latter view which has led some universities to try to introduce entrepreneurship to a wide range of subjects. It may be interesting to note that this lack of clarity has even been seen to be beneficial as indicated by a UK Department of Education and Employment official writing in 1995 about the Enterprise in Higher Education (EHE) initiative:

> The idea of enterprise has not always been uniformly welcomed by academics. . . . The title 'enterprise' was not initially helpful, being perceived by some as striking at established values and practices and challenging the cultures of some traditional discipline areas. Nevertheless, the very lack of clarity of the title allowed universities the scope to creatively reinterpret and accommodate 'enterprise', the better to match institutional strengths and priorities. Thus a strong institutional commitment to negotiated contract aims and objectives has generally been secured without unduly offending the liberal values prevailing. EHE goes with the grain insofar as it often enables or accelerates developments which HEIs would have wished themselves to implement.[39]

Therefore there has not been a clear and consistent academic view on what entrepreneurship is. As described earlier a variety of different approaches have been taken in teaching it, possibly on the basis that 'the customer is always right', and in researching it there is always a temptation to follow the meanings assumed by the providers of the research funding. As a result, as one observer has put it: 'sixty years of research is yet to produce widespread agreement on how to define entrepreneurship'.[40]

Box 3.3   Observation or wishful thinking?

It is clear that Cantillon used the term 'entrepreneur' as a label for what he saw as a distinct category of economic activity. However, some others seem to want to use the term 'entrepreneur', not as a label for what they have seen, but as an indication of what they would like to see as a distinguishable economic activity. For instance, it seems that some of those who want to see more business start-ups define entrepreneurs as people who start businesses. Having unilaterally fixed the meaning of the word to cover only the things which they want it to be, they are then tempted to assume that everything to which that label is applied must be what they want. Therefore they expect that people who receive entrepreneurship training will then become the entrepreneurs they want and start the businesses they hope to see. This is, therefore, a form of wishful thinking which does seem to affect some official observations.

Measuring entrepreneurship – and the potential for confusion

Both to justify or monitor and evaluate government entrepreneurship programmes and to provide baseline data for research, there is a requirement to identify and assess on a consistent basis the number or proportion of entrepreneurs in a country or region. There is also a strong preference for doing this inexpensively, which usually means doing it by using readily available data – such as new firm registrations or self-employment statistics. Shane, for instance, refers to new firm formation and self-employment as 'operational definitions of entrepreneurship' which are used in empirical research because other definitions are 'difficult to operationalize',[41] but, because the varied government, academic and statistical interests in entrepreneurship do not share a consistent definition of what entrepreneurship is, this can lead to confusion. The following are examples:

Self-employed people can be equated with business owners

It is relatively easy to label, identify and/or count people who are classified as self-employed, and who are then presumed to be the proprietors of recognised businesses, so this is the definition of entrepreneurship which is often de facto adopted by researchers because other definitions are too difficult for practical use.

The distinction between employee and the self-employed is relatively recent

But there may not be much difference between supposedly self-employed people and employees. A freelance of the medieval period would today be classed as a self-employed contractor, although, if he remained in one army for long enough, the tax authorities might class him as employed. However, the distinction between being an employee and being a self-employed contractor, such as a freelance, came much later than the medieval period.

Counting start-up businesses instead of entrepreneurs

Because the number of new businesses can be ascertained relatively easily from business registration records, new business formation rates can be quoted to indicate levels of entrepreneurship – and this approach is attractive because new business formation is often the declared aim of entrepreneurship policy. However, using the number of businesses can also be problematic for those who want to know the number of entrepreneurs because a business can be started by more than one person or the same person can start more than one business – and a business can change its legal form without any real change in its activity.

An assumption that the people who will start high-growth businesses can be targeted

In order to encourage the creation of significant numbers of new jobs (and especially high-value-added exporting jobs), governments and others want to focus their interest and support on high-growth businesses – which are often assumed to be high-tech. Therefore, as a sub-set of the job-creation interest, there is a focus on those people who will create and run such businesses, and to assume, that, by defining entrepreneurs in that way, they can thus target them.

Box 3.4   The GEM approach

The Global Entrepreneurship Monitor (GEM) initiative has aims which have included assessing the extent to which the level of entrepreneurial activity affects a country's rate of economic growth and prosperity. Therefore GEM has wanted a measure of entrepreneurship which can be used to compare the rates of entrepreneurship in different countries and which can easily be applied in a simple telephone survey. Thus, in conformation to the narrower business interpretation of entrepreneurship, GEM has defined it as 'any attempt to create a new business enterprise or to expand an existing business by an individual, a team of individuals or an established business'[42] and estimates the level of involvement in early-stage entrepreneurial activity – its Total Entrepreneurial Activity (TEA) index – by combining the prevalence rate of nascent entrepreneurs (those individuals between the ages of 18 and 64 years, who have taken some action towards creating a new business in the past year) and new business owners (individuals who are active as owner-managers of a new business that has paid wages or salaries for more than 3 months, but less than 42 months).[43] GEM thus uses a combination of action for new business formation and engagement in managing a new business as its main measure of entrepreneurship.

Other developments

Among other developments which have been supposed to have an impact on the prevalence of entrepreneurship, and thus on where it might be observed, are the following:

• *The world order is changing.* In the second half of the 20th century one of the impacts of Fordism was that many people in the more developed countries expected to be able to find employment for life in a large business (or in the state bureaucracy). Although for those growing up in that period this may have seemed to be the norm, from a historical perspective it only applied for a short period. Now large businesses are changing and jobs for life are far fewer. People must therefore expect to have to take more responsibility for identifying new employment opportunities during their working lives. This can be described as being entrepreneurial and, indeed, Audretsch et al. call Toffler's third wave 'the entrepreneurial economy'.[44]

- *Social entrepreneurship.* The third sector – that part of an economy which is not part of either the public or the private sector – has recently been receiving greater recognition. Although there has been third-sector activity for as long as there has been distinguishable public- and private-sector activity, it has not received as much recognition. At least in part this has been because there was a lack of words to describe it. Now a vocabulary is emerging, and among the phrases being used in this context are the terms 'social economy', 'social enterprise', 'social entrepreneur' and 'social entrepreneurship'. The 'social economy' is sometimes considered to refer to either the whole of the third sector or at least to that part of it which is composed of co-operatives, mutuals, associations and foundations. Those sorts of organisations are also often referred to as 'social enterprises' because they are organisations with a social purpose which are not primarily funded by the state but nevertheless have to generate enough income to survive – although there is no widely accepted single definition of them. Then the people who start and run such social enterprises can be referred to as 'social entrepreneurs' – people who are entrepreneurial in starting and maintaining enterprises which exist primarily to deliver a social benefit rather than to make money for individuals.

Popular perceptions

The observations on entrepreneurship summarised earlier come largely from informed and/or professional people often in branches of academia or government. Therefore they might be supposed to be considered and often reasoned views on what is or isn't entrepreneurship. However, views on entrepreneurship are not confined to such people. There is considerable public discussion of entrepreneurs, and many people have a view on them. Those views may not be well informed or thought through, and often they are not systematically or diligently recorded but, nevertheless, they are influential because they are widely held.

Essentially those views, and the people who hold them, might be grouped under two headings. On the one hand there are those who, if they think about entrepreneurs, identify them as special people who have a sort of immutable characteristic which, although possessed by just a relatively few people, nevertheless enables them to make an important economic contribution. On the other hand there are those who appear to consider entrepreneurship to be a socially harmful activity which embodies the core negative aspects of capitalism. These might be called the 'heroic' or 'villainous' views of entrepreneurs and are expounded on later, although they are not necessarily mutually exclusive. Also, as Box 3.5 indicates, such views are not equally distributed but appear to be culturally influenced and therefore more prominent in some countries than others.

'Heroic' entrepreneurs

Many people appear to have a view of entrepreneurs as typified by people such as Steve Jobs, Mark Zuckerberg, Bill Gates, Alan Sugar and Richard Branson – not least because they often seem to get lots of public notice. These are individuals who appear to be self-starters and often seem to operate in the ICT sector. They are admired and even envied for their ability – seemingly effortlessly – to amass fortunes. Thus they have been described as 'heroic entrepreneurs' who are distinctly different from 'normal' people – and it seems to be assumed that they must be born that way and therefore others, who have not been born with those attributes, won't be able do it however much they try to emulate them. As expounded in one article about them:

> It is ironic that one of the biggest academic growth industries in recent years has been the study of what makes entrepreneurs tick. . . . Yet no real entrepreneur actually believes entrepreneurial skills are learnable or transferable. You're either an entrepreneur or you're not. It's a state of being, not a trade or a vocation.[45]

That quote may be somewhat old, and often people now recognise that entrepreneurs are not usually lone operators. For instance, Cooney observes that 'one of the great myths of entrepreneurship has been the notion of the entrepreneur as a lone hero'.[46] Nevertheless, as stated, for instance, by Drakopoulou Dodd and Anderson, 'the idea of the entrepreneur operating as an atomistic individual – sometimes maverick, often non-conforming, but single-handedly relentlessly pursuing opportunity – is an ideological convenience': a notion which persists despite 'considerable evidence to the contrary'.[47]

'Villainous' entrepreneurs

However, the lone or 'heroic' entrepreneur is not always seen as having a positive influence, and some people view an entrepreneur as being someone who is, in the main, motivated primarily by personal greed and is able and willing to dissemble and cheat to get what he or she wants. They dislike what they think they see and appear to view entrepreneurship as, at best, a questionable activity in which respectable people should not engage. For instance, it has been said of entrepreneurship education that 'there seems to be an assumption among some folks that entrepreneurship is simply a self-serving pursuit that only teaches students how to maximise their own wealth at the expense of others'.[48]

Some go as far as to see this as being symptomatic of what they believe are the inherent excesses of capitalism and think entrepreneurs typify and/or are responsible for those defects. Those who think it wrong that some individuals should accumulate much more wealth than others often vilify those who do amass fortunes through business (but sometimes do not seem to treat high-earning pop musicians or footballers similarly) and identify them as entrepreneurs and assume that (almost) all entrepreneurs use what are, at best, questionable practices mainly for the purpose of their own personal enrichment at the expense of others. An example of such a view was given by Jiang Zemin, who in 1989, shortly after becoming general secretary of the Communist Party, the most powerful position in China, was reported to have 'summarised the party's suspicion of entrepreneurs by characterising them as "self-employed traders and peddlers [who] cheat, embezzle, bribe and evade taxation"'.[49]

Box 3.5   Different social constructions of entrepreneurship

De Koning and Drakopoulou Dodd have examined international similarities and differences in social constructions of the entrepreneur. To do this they compared the metaphors used in newspaper articles about entrepreneurship over a 10-week period (from December 2001 to February 2002) in a selection of nationally distributed English-language newspapers in Australia, Canada, India, Ireland, UK and the United States.

In their study they found 'no monoliths of meaning' – but instead that 'multiple, contested, fragmented, contradictory, ambiguous, malleable, slippery meanings . . . are ubiquitous' and this

> is evident within data for every country, for every newspaper, and, in many cases, within individual articles. Importantly, an element in this multiplex and sometimes contradictory concept is a contrast between positive appreciations of entrepreneurship, being held consistently against the shadow of entrepreneurship's dark side.

The authors report that although there were some broad patterns of surface-level similarity across the cultures studied, there are country-specific idiosyncrasies and examples of the same metaphor carrying strongly divergent meanings in one country than it does in another. For instance:

- Gambling metaphors are common in five of the six countries, but 'in Ireland and Canada gambling was only associated with losing and was an unmistakably negative narrative'.
- 'In general the Irish material shows a certain degree of cynicism toward the mythic rags-to-riches self-made man narrative.'
- In the UK and Canada the entrepreneur, 'although necessary for economic development, is seen as a dangerous outsider, a greedy, shady and selfish transgressor of social norms', and the UK metaphors describe entrepreneurs as 'pugnacious, and fighting hard and dirty'.
- In Canadian discourse especially, the entrepreneur can be seen 'as a social outcast' and 'the general picture which emerges from the Canadian articles is of the entrepreneurs as a dangerous unstable outsider bringing unwelcome disruption and justifiably liable to dramatic personal and commercial shame.'
- In contrast in Australia, the entrepreneur is portrayed as a 'swashbuckling hero, whose rational decision making and aggression are key and valued elements in business success . . . Overall the Australian sample texts paint a picture of the entrepreneur as a glamorous, exciting, aggressive, manly figure'.
- In the United States the emphasis is on 'the morally perfect legend of the little guy who wins out . . . by dint of vision, hard work and integrity'.
- The Indian perception places weight on 'the need for external support [and] collective action'.

Source: Based on A. de Koning and S. Drakopoulou Dodd, 'The Entrepreneurial Kaleidoscope: International Social Construction of the Entrepreneur – A Metaphorical Study', Paper presented at the *36th ISBE Conference*, Cardiff, November 2013.

In conclusion

This chapter indicates and exemplifies the variety of views on entrepreneurs and entrepreneurship – but it does not seek to quantify or, at this stage, criticise them. Also it has left out many relevant and important observations. However, the intention is not to try to cover everything but to indicate the diversity of views about entrepreneurship and to identify, in the context of the history of work presented in Chapter 2, the evolution of many of the different perceptions of entrepreneurship which now abound.

Notes

1 *Oxford English Dictionary* (London: Book Club Associates, 1979), p. 879.
2 L. J. Filion, 'Defining the entrepreneur', in L.-P. Dana (ed), *World Encyclopedia of Entrepreneurship* (Cheltenham: Edward Elgar, 2011), pp. 41–52.
3 R. Cantillon, *Essai sur la nature du commerce en général*, Edited with an English translation and other material by H. Higgs (London: Frank Cass & Co Ltd, 1959 – reissued for the Royal Economic Society).
4 Ibid., p. 49.
5 See for example H. Higgs, 'Life and work of Richard Cantillon', in R. Cantillon (ed), Op Cit, p. 383.
6 W. K. Bolton and J. L. Thompson, *Entrepreneurs: Talent, Temperament, Technique* (Oxford: Butterworth-Heinmann, 2000), p. 261.
7 W. J. Baumol, 'Entrepreneurship: Productive, Unproductive, and Destructive', *Journal of Political Economy*, Vol.98 No.5, pt.1, 1990, p. 897.
8 Ibid., p. 893.
9 Ibid., pp. 893–921.
10 Ibid., p. 894.
11 J. A. Schumpeter, *The Theory of Economic Development* (Leipzig: Bunker and Humblot, 1912, English edition Cambridge, MA: Harvard University Press, 1934), p. 66.
12 D. C. McClelland, *The Achieving Society* (Princeton, NJ: D. Van Nostrand Company Inc., 1961), p. 205.
13 R. F. Hébert and A. N. Link, *A History of Entrepreneurship* (Abingdon: Routledge, 2009), p. 24.
14 A. H. Cole, 'Entrepreneurship as an Area of Research', *The Journal of Economic History*, Vol.2 supplement, 1942, pp. 118–126.
15 J. A. Katz, 'The Chronology and Intellectual Trajectory of American Entrepreneurship Education 1876–1999', *Journal of Business Venturing*, Vol.18 No.2, 2003, p. 283.
16 J. Storey, *Understanding the Small Business Sector* (London: Routledge, 1994), p. 113.
17 NESTA, *The Vital 6 Percent* (London: NESTA, 2009).
18 P. Urwin, *Self-Employment, Small Firms and Enterprise* (London: Institute of Economic Affairs in association with Profile Books Ltd., 2011), pp. 107–108.
19 R. Botham and S. Bridge, 'NESTA's Vital (or not so vital?) Six Percent', paper presented at the *35*th *ISBE Conference*, Dublin, November 2012.
20 Invest Northern Ireland, *Corporate Plan 2008–2011*, www.investmi.com (accessed 11 February 2009), p. 5.
21 National Agency for Enterprise and Construction, *Entrepreneurship Index 2006: Entrepreneurship Conditions in Denmark*, November 2006, www.foranet.dk (accessed 16 March 2009), p. 5.
22 H.M. Gabr and A. Hoffmann, *A General Policy Framework for Entrepreneurship*, FORA (Copenhagen, Denmark: Ministry of Economic and Business Affairs' Division for Research and Analysis, April 2006).

23 Scottish Enterprise, *Enterprise and Economic Growth*, SEBPC(08)01, www. scottish-enterprise.com (accessed 15 February 2009).

24 The *Entrepreneurship and Education Action Plan*, published in March 2003, a joint plan developed by the Department of Enterprise Trade, and Investment (DETI, the Department of Education (DE) and the Department for Employment and Learning (DEL).

25 Said, for instance, by Lord Young, the UK Secretary of State for Employment, during a celebrity lecture in Northern Ireland, May 1993.

26 Scottish Government, *Scotland's Economic Strategy* (Edinburgh: Scottish Government, March 2015), p. 52.

27 P. Hannon, 'Philosophies of Enterprise and Entrepreneurship Education and the Challenges for Higher Education in the UK', *International Journal of Entrepreneurship and Innovation*, Vol.6 No.2, 2005, pp. 105–114.

28 U. Hytti and P. Kuopusjärvi, 'Three Perspectives to Evaluating Entrepreneurship Education: Evaluators, Programme Promoters and Policy Makers', paper presented at the *efmd 34th EISB Conference*, Turku, 2004, based on *Evaluating and Measuring Entrepreneurship and Enterprise Education*, Small Business Institute, Turku, Finland, 2004 – from a Leonardo funded project.

29 D. Jasinski, 'A New Approach to Integrated Entrepreneurship Education', paper presented at the *ICSB 48th World Conference*, Belfast, 2003.

30 K. Mole, 'Introduction', in K. Mole and M. Ram (eds), *Perspectives in Entrepreneurship* (Basingstoke: Palgrave Macmillan, 2012), p. 3.

31 J. Curran and J. Stanworth, 'Education and Training for Enterprise: Some Problems of Classification, Evaluation, Policy and Research', *International Small Business Journal*, Vol.7 No.2, 1989, p. 12.

32 S. Shane, *A General Theory of Entrepreneurship* (Cheltenham: Edward Elgar, 2003), p. 4.

33 J. A. Timmons, *The Entrepreneurial Mind* (Andover, MA: Brick House Publishing, 1989), p. 1.

34 A. A. Gibb, 'SME Policy, Academic Research and the Growth of Ignorance, Mythical Concepts, Myths, Assumptions, Rituals and Confusions', *International Small Business Journal*, Vol.18 No.3, 2000, p. 16.

35 Reported in H. H. Stevenson, 'Intellectual Foundations of Entrepreneurship', in H. P. Welsch (ed), *Entrepreneurship: The Way Ahead*, (New York and London: Routledge, 2004), p. 3.

36 A. A. Gibb, 'The Enterprise Culture and Education: Understanding Enterprise Education and its Links with Small Business, Entrepreneurship and Wider Educational Goals', *International Small Business Journal*, Vol.11 No.3, 1993, pp. 11–34.

37 P. Hannon, Op Cit, p. 108.

38 U. Hytti and P. Kuopusjärvi, Op Cit.

39 T. Whitely, 'Enterprise in Higher Education – An Overview from the Department for Education and Employment', *Education + Training*, Vol.37 No.9, 1995.

40 H. Lewis, 'A Systems Approach to the Complexity of Entrepreneurship Education', paper presented at the *30th ISBA National Small Firms Conference*, Glasgow, 2007.

41 S. Shane, *A General Theory of Entrepreneurship* (Cheltenham: Edward Elgar, 2003), p. 5.

42 A. L. Zacharakis, W. D. Bygrave and D. A. Shepherd, *Global Entrepreneurship Monitor United States of America 2000 Executive Report* (Kansas City, MO:

Kauffman Centre for Entrepreneurial Leadership at the Ewing Marion Kauff-mann Foundation, 2000), p. 5.

43 Based on N. Bosma and R. Harding, *Global Entrepreneurship Monitor GEM 2006 Results* (London: Babson College and London Business School, 2007), p. 9.

44 D. B. Audretsch, A. R. Thurik and E. Stam, *Unraveling the Shift to the Entrepreneurial Economy* (Zoetermeer, Netherlands: EIM, 2011).

45 M. Brown, 'Risky Business', in *Holland Herald* (the in-flight magazine of KLM).

46 T. Cooney, 'Editorial: What Is an Entrepreneurial Team?', *International Small Business Journal*, Vol.23 No.3, 2005, p. 226.

47 S. Drakopoulou Dodd and A. Anderson, 'Mumpsimus and the Mything of the Individualistic Entrepreneur', *International Small Business Journal*, Vol.25 No.4, August 2007, pp. 341–358.

48 J. Cornwall, *The Entrepreneurship Educator Newsletter*, 30 May 2012, www.planningshop.com.

49 D. Acemoglu and J. A. Robinson, *Why Nations Fail* (London: Profile Books, 2013), p. 438.

4 Reflections on what has been found

So far, in Chapter 1, this book indicates that a strong impetus to our search for entrepreneurship has come from governments. Because they believe that entrepreneurship is the condition which generates entrepreneurs, who in turn create the businesses which provide employment and other economic benefits, they want more entrepreneurship. Therefore, to help them develop polices for getting more of it, they seek some understanding of what entrepreneurship is and what might influence it.

Entrepreneurship is identified primarily in the word of work. Chapter 2 therefore provides a brief history of work and a description of how some of its various forms may have evolved, and Chapter 3 then indicates where, in that evolution, observers have identified entrepreneurs and entrepreneurship. However, although that chapter indicates that entrepreneurs have often been observed and/or described, this chapter suggests they have not often been defined. On the other hand entrepreneurship has been defined but often only by describing the activities of entrepreneurs – and its presence only inferred from their existence. Further an analysis of the different observations and/or identifications of entrepreneurs suggests that there are at least ten different perceptions of what an entrepreneur is – just as there are many different definitions of entrepreneurship.

This chapter therefore explores these different perceptions – what they are and why they might have arisen. It also looks at some of the responses to that apparent variety and the attempts that have been made to explain it and suggests an alternative conclusion.

Different perceptions of entrepreneurs

As Chapter 3 indicates, there is a long history of different perceptions of an entrepreneur going back almost to the first use of the word in this context by Cantillon, and a single, acceptable, definitive definition of it has long been sought but still not been agreed on. In a paper written in 1988 Gartner quoted Cole as suggesting in 1969 that 'for ten years we tried to define the entrepreneur [but] we never succeeded'. Gartner himself then presented a summary of twenty-nine views on entrepreneurs, twenty-one of which included some sort of a definition,[1] and another review conducted some 25 year later found more than twenty typologies and associated descriptions of the entrepreneur that had been offered by researchers.[2] In its survey of entrepreneurship Chapter 3 does not present a picture of all of these variations, but, nevertheless, it is possible from it to identify a number of categories of people for whom, at one time or another, the word entrepreneur has been used as a label. Here, for example, are summaries of ten of them:

1   *Someone operating economically at risk.* The Irish expatriate Cantillon identified the entrepreneur as an individual operating economically at risk. It is interesting that a similar view is suggested in a recent Irish policy review which suggests that an interpretation of the word entrepreneur is an occupational motion which may be defined as 'working for one's own account and risk'.[3]

2   *An innovator – and creative destroyer.* After Cantillon, Say's subsequent interpretation was that an entrepreneur was someone who innovated by introducing to the market something new such as a new product, or service, or a new process – which is likely to result in some form of 'creative destruction' which he thus identified as a salient feature of entrepreneurship. Baumol et al., in their book on capitalism, focus on the innovative part of this when they suggest that the term entrepreneur should refer to someone who develops 'any entity, new or existing, that provides a new product or service or that develops and uses new methods to produce or deliver existing goods and services at lower cost'.[4]

3   *An enterprising person and a self-starter.* A wider interpretation of an entrepreneur, and an extrapolation of Cantillon's meaning, is that he or she is a 'change-maker' who will be proactive in doing things. This interpretation often emphasises the self-employment outcome rather than the realisation of any other goals – in which case it can be summarised as job making rather than job taking. However, a person can be enterprising in any activity, even if it isn't a business, and in this category 'entrepreneurs are, in essence, individuals who take action to convert their ideas into reality'.[5]

4   *An ingenious self-advancer.* Many commentators have not actually offered a definition of an entrepreneur. However one who has is Baumol (see Box 3.1) who, in one variation, defined 'entrepreneurs . . . simply, to be persons who are ingenious and creative in finding ways that add to their own wealth, power, and prestige'.[6]

5   *A 'heroic', compulsive venturer.* A common perception of the entrepreneur is that he, or sometimes she, is the sort of person who is born that way and is almost inevitably going to start and run their own

business venture – whatever other people may think of them or the level of the need or of encouragement and/or support for doing it. In this they are thus supposed to be clearly distinguishable from non-entrepreneurs who don't create businesses.

6   *A selfish near-criminal.* An extension of the compulsive entrepreneur model is the view held by some people that an entrepreneur is someone who is prepared to engage in questionable, or even clearly criminal, business practices for personal enrichment. Sometimes entrepreneur-ship is shunned as being socially undesirable and/or inferior and, from this perspective, entrepreneurs are seen as parasites on the efforts of others and as scourges on good society (see also Box 4.1).

7   *A business owner.* Although there is a clear understanding that 'not every new small business is entrepreneurial or represents entrepreneur-ship',[7] nevertheless sometimes the assumption is made that anyone who starts (and runs and/or grows) a business or businesses is an entrepre-neur. A typical view is that 'an entrepreneur is anyone who starts his or her own business',[8] and this is a particularly convenient assumption for researchers and statisticians seeking to measure the level of entrepre-neurship. It is often relatively easy to assess the number of businesses from existing databases, whereas other interpretations of entrepreneur-ship are much harder to use.

8   *A self-employed person.* A problem with equating entrepreneurs with business owners is that some entrepreneurs start more than one busi-ness, and sometimes several entrepreneurs are involved in the same business. An alternative approach sometimes adopted by statisticians (and others) is to assume that anyone who is classified as self-employed can be counted as an entrepreneur, even if it is a one-person business and/or if the person concerned works on a freelance basis – into which they might have been more or less forced by a former employer's desire to reduce direct employment. Despite informed comments such as 'most self-employed are not and do not self-report to be entrepreneur-ial',[9] an incentive for making such assumptions is the relatively easy availability of data about the numbers of people who are categorised as self-employed.

9   *A source of jobs (and/or of economic growth).* It would seem that often the main, or at least the initial, reason why governments are interested in entrepreneurs is the belief that they create new, and often small, busi-nesses which are the main source of new jobs and make other contribu-tions to economic growth. As it is these economic contributions that are the governments' main objective, those working in government often tend to view entrepreneurs in that context and assume that, even if it is not their prime function, it is at least their main output and even an aspi-

ration that they all share. Thus, by extension, they seem to believe that entrepreneurs and/or the businesses that they create have a job creation and/or a growth imperative.

10 *A source of high-tech, high-growth businesses.* A version of the previous meaning is the tendency to define entrepreneurs as people who start (and run and/or grow) high-tech and/or high-growth businesses – because there is a desire for more such businesses. However, it appears that in some quarters it has even been supposed that such a distinguishable group of people exists and that it is appropriate to try to reserve the label 'entrepreneurs' for them.

Box 4.1   Negative attitudes to entrepreneurs

People who engage in business have not always been held in high regard. As Baumol has indicated (see Box 3.1), those in the higher levels of Roman society considered trade or similar forms of business to be a socially unacceptable or inferior activity and it is clear that, before them, in classical Athens market traders were often viewed, and portrayed in comedies, as cheats and rogues.[10] Indeed in a society such as that of the Greeks, which accepted slavery as the norm, work generally was not something to be undertaken by honourable people:

> Part of the point of warfare and conquest was enslavement of the enemy. . . . Little wonder, therefore, that labour was seen as dishonourable. It was associated with defeat and permanent social inferiority.[11]

Thus, since the days of ancient Greece, aristocrats have often seen money as the embodiment of corruption, and they have distained the market and tried to set themselves apart from those who engaged in the seemingly sordid world of commercial exchange.[12]

Even today there are many who consider money to be the root of all evil and therefore also distrust these whose activities seem to make money. Burns, in writing about entrepreneurship, reports 'an old adage that if you scratch an entrepreneur you find a "spiv" (somebody who makes a living from unlawful work)',[13] and Cornwall, in his entrepreneurship education newsletter, has reported that 'there seems to be an assumption among some folks that entrepreneurship is simply a self-serving pursuit that only teaches students how to maximise their own wealth at the expense of others'.[14]

Different definitions of entrepreneurship

The different identifications of an entrepreneur listed earlier include relatively few attempts at a definition. Instead what has been defined much more often, either directly or by implication, is entrepreneurship, and the observations considered in Chapter 3 reveal a wide variety of such definitions. Here is a selection, roughly going from the broader to the narrower:

1   The definition ascribed to Harvard which is that 'entrepreneurship is the pursuit of opportunity beyond the resources you currently control'.[15]

2   Gibb's indicated interpretation that

> entrepreneurship relates to ways in which people, in all kinds of organisations behave in order to cope with and take advantage of uncertainty and complexity and how in turn this becomes embodied in: ways of doing things; ways of seeing things; ways of feeling things; ways of communicating things; and ways of learning things.[16]

3   The Northern Ireland government's Entrepreneurship and Education Action Plan indicated that for the plan, entrepreneurship was considered to be 'the ability of an individual, possessing a range of essential skills and attributes, to make a unique, innovative and creative contribution in the world of work, whether in employment or self-employment'.[17]

4   Hytti and Kuopusjärvi's[18] suggestion that there are three different roles which might be assigned to entrepreneurship education programmes depending on what aim was being pursued, and one of the aims they identify is to learn to become entrepreneurial – an approach which is consistent with a wider interpretation of entrepreneurship.

5   Baumol, who, as indicated earlier, defined 'entrepreneurs . . . simply, to be persons who are ingenious and creative in finding ways that add to their own wealth, power, and prestige',[19] implied that entrepreneurship therefore refers to such people operating in any area of life. However, he also indicated that, on occasion and by implication, entrepreneurship has been defined as a significant contribution to economic growth when he reported that:

> Where [economic] growth has slowed, it is implied that a decline in entrepreneurship was partly to blame . . . At another time and place, it is said, the flowering of entrepreneurship accounts for unprecedented expansion.[20]

6 In 1988 Low and MacMillan, in looking at the purpose of entrepreneurship research and having reviewed a number of definitions suggested that 'entrepreneurship be defined as the "creation of new enterprise" and . . . that entrepreneurship research [should] seek to explain and facilitate the role of new enterprise in furthering economic progress'.[21]

7 Shane's definition of entrepreneurship as 'an activity that involves the discovery, evaluation and exploitation of opportunities to introduce new goods and services, ways of organising, markets, processes and raw materials through organising efforts that previously had not existed'.[22]

8 An American commentator's assertion was that 'one of the major objectives of entrepreneurship education is to provide students with the necessary skills to design, create, launch and effectively manage a business'.[23]

9 Another of the aims Hytti and Kuopusjärvi[24] identified for entrepreneurship education programmes is that of learning to become an entrepreneur – which is generally interpreted as learning how to start a business.

10 GEM's definition of entrepreneurship has been 'any attempt to create a new business enterprise or to expand an existing business by an individual, a team of individuals or an established business'.[25]

11 Invest Northern Ireland declared in 2008 that its Accelerating Entrepreneurship Strategy 'will increasingly emphasise the acceleration of high-potential existing and start-up companies . . . (to) provide the supply line for future exports based on new product and process innovation'.[26] Similarly a Danish entrepreneurship initiative defined entrepreneurship specifically as 'the entry and creation of high-growth firms'.[27]

These descriptions or definitions of entrepreneurship are presented in a sequence which indicates they have a wide spectrum of meanings from the relatively broad encompassing almost any enterprising activity to the very narrow in which entrepreneurship is used to refer just to the creation of a limited range of businesses. This is echoed in the suggestion by Bridge (indicated in Box 4.2) that the spectrum of different interpretations of enterprise or entrepreneurship could be divided into different categories which might be identified by 'E' numbers.

Box 4.2   E-numbers: interpretation and some comparable uses

Bridge has suggested using E-numbers to distinguish different positions on the spectrum of meanings of enterprise or entrepreneurship from broad to narrow.

E-number	Interpretation	Comparable uses?
E0	The application of enterprise attributes in any context, for instance, in sport, exploration or art.	Broader definitions of enterprise
E1	The application of enterprising attributes for the economic advancement of self and/or others, but not necessarily as a business (for instance, in employment or in unproductive or even destructive entrepreneurship).	Baumol NI Entrepreneurship and Education Action Plan Social enterprise
E2	The formation of any new economic venture (or its subsequent growth), including self-employment and me-too businesses.	Birch GEM Social entrepreneurship
E3	The formation and/or growth of novel private-sector business ventures, i.e. ventures which are a distinct development of what already exists.	The target of much entrepreneurship policy
E4	The formation and/or growth of new, innovative, high-tech, fast-growth, high-added-value, knowledge-intensive, exporting business ventures.	Gazelles, HPSUs Invest NI and Danish uses
E5	Could there be narrower definitions – for instance, with the same focus as E4 but limited only to certain targeted sectors?	

Source: Based on S. Bridge, *Rethinking Enterprise Policy* (Basingstoke: Palgrave Macmillan, 2010), p. 107.

Why there are different perceptions/definitions

These views or perceptions may not all be equally common or influential, but nevertheless they exist and are reflective of the lack of clarity that pervades the entrepreneurship search. They also raise the question of why there should be so many different views, especially if, as many people appear to assume, entrepreneurship is essentially one phenomenon.

The following paragraphs suggest possible reasons for that variety. Even if entrepreneurship is essentially one phenomenon, it is clear that people are looking at it in different ways and from different perspectives. For instance, as indicated later, government perceptions of entrepreneurship might be influenced by considerations of jobs and measurement, academic perceptions influenced by budgets and public perceptions influenced by the media and political views. Also some reported views are clearly based on observed reality, whereas others appear to be more the product of wishful thinking of what people want to see.

Causes or effects

One reason for the different perspectives is that some of the people who have identified entrepreneurship have focused on the supposed activity of entrepreneurs and others on the outcomes from that activity. Cantillon is an example of someone observing the activity itself, whereas those who focus on the businesses or the jobs created are looking essentially at the supposed outcomes of entrepreneurial activity. Creative destruction is clearly an outcome, and even registered self-employment is the result of activity, not its cause. It is, of course, often possible to identify something by its outcomes. Acids can be distinguished from alkalis by their different effects on litmus paper, and in medicine the presence of some diseases can best be diagnosed by detecting in a patient's blood the specific antibodies, the production of which the diseases are known to trigger. However, identifications based on effects are different from those based on direct observation of the causes, and there is always the possibility that the supposed link is not there or that the same effect could be produced by more than one cause.

Box 4.3   Causes and effects

Often it is effects which are noticed first and trigger attempts to identify causes, but not always successfully. For instance, in the history of medicine observations of the effects of illness have led to various suggestions about its cause:

- The early ideas of illness and disease considered it all as *dis-ease* and did not distinguish between what we now see as different causes, such as germs, diet deficiencies or poisons.
- It was observations of the body which led to the four humours theory, with the suggestion that a humour imbalance caused illnesses. Thus the treatment of fevers by bleeding, on the assumption that it was having too much blood which made patients hot and wet, was an evidence-based policy. It was only later that the discovery of circulation of blood helped to distinguished it from the other humours.

- The importance of cleanliness in surgery and the possibility of vaccination had both become apparent before the discovery of germs explained why they worked.
- At one time malaria (mal air) and other diseases such as cholera were thought to be spread by bad air – and London's sewers were originally built to take away the sources of such smells. It was only the discovery first of the importance of cleanliness and then the identification of invasive organisms (bacteria and viruses) and their transmission mechanisms (e.g. cholera is water-borne and malaria is spread by mosquitoes) which changed this view.
- And in medicine the placebo effect means that even a potentially harmful treatment can still have a positive effect if the patient believes in it.

Reality or wishful thinking

An example of a focus on effects, not causes, is an apparent tendency by some people to define entrepreneurship by the effects they want it to produce. Thus their identifications of entrepreneurship seem to be based, not on observations of the reality of the actions or outputs of entrepreneurs, but on wishful thinking about their impacts. Cantillon's identification was based on observations of reality, and he appears to have applied the word entrepreneur as a label for a form of economic behaviour he had seen and was thus making an objective judgement that the behaviour exists rather than forming a subjective view that he wanted it to exist. However, the starting point for others appears to be a wish for the supposed outcomes and thus a desire to identify the people supposedly responsible for them. For instance, the instigators of the Danish initiative which defined entrepreneurship specifically as 'the entry and creation of high-growth firms'[28] seem to have based their view, not on an observation that people identified as entrepreneurs only created high-growth businesses, but on a desire for more high-growth businesses and thus a wish that that was indeed what entrepreneurs did. Those who thus identify entrepreneurship based on wishful thinking are focusing primarily on the effects of entrepreneurship: on the outcomes they want it to produce rather than the nature of the activity which leads to those outcomes.

Different purposes

If, when they identify entrepreneurs and entrepreneurship, some people are engaging in wishful thinking, whether consciously or not, that is because they have a specific objective in mind. For whatever reason they have a requirement which they are trying to address, and they have come to understand that entrepreneurship could help deliver at least part of the response. However, they do not necessarily all have the same agenda and are not therefore all looking for the same outcomes. Their views of entrepreneurship will therefore be affected by what they are trying to achieve. For instance, if governments have a desire for more jobs and an understanding that entrepreneurs create businesses which in turn create jobs, that leads to a perception that entrepreneurship has a job-creation potential and can be identified by that outcome. Thus, identifying entrepreneurship in terms of jobs or high-growth businesses can reflect an employment or business growth objective, and identifying the self-employed or business owners as entrepreneurs can be the result, not of a fundamental belief that entrepreneurs and the self-employed and/or business owners are always the same thing, but of a requirement for a measurement and a realisation that self-employment or business ownership can relatively easily be counted.

Propaganda

Another source of, or reason for, different perspectives is that there are different received views of what entrepreneurs are. If we identify entrepreneurship in a particular way because that is how we have been taught to identify it, then that leads us to see what we think we should see, not what is actually there. Thus identifications of entrepreneurs as either heroes and villains can come, not from close observation of the activities of independently identified entrepreneurs, but from a received understanding that that is what entrepreneurs are like, often reinforced by a consequent and self-reinforcing tendency to identify as entrepreneurs only the people who behave in the expected way. We see what others encourage us to see.

Responses to this variety

The suggestions given earlier are some of the reasons why there may be different perceptions and, consequently, different identifications and/or definitions of entrepreneurs and/or entrepreneurship. However, although they may help to explain why there are differences, they do not help to reconcile them. Those differences remain, and if they are to be resolved and/or removed, other approaches are required. Essentially it would seem three responses have been tried – which might be summarised as ignore, core and explore.

Ignore

There appear in the literature to be relatively few comments on the proliferation of different views about entrepreneurship, and that could be because the form of response which most people seem to take is to try to ignore the differences. Failing to notice inconvenient truths is a common human failing and often the path of least resistance because, as in this case, acknowledging such an issue would appear to require too many adjustments.

Core

An alternative response which does not ignore the different perceptions and interpretations of entrepreneurship is the belief that there is a core behaviour which is entrepreneurship, with the rest being something else, albeit possibly related. The following is one reflection of this core view that was formulated when enterprise, rather than entrepreneurship, was the preferred description:

> Broadly . . . the label enterprise might be applied when:
>
> * the task is non-routine
> * the task is somewhat complex
> * the task is goal directed
> * the goal(s) are demanding but attainable
>
> and when:
>
> * the task is tackled in an adventurous manner
> * the task is approached in a determined and dynamic manner
> * the task accomplishes the set goals (or comes near to so doing?).[29]

The implication of this approach is that the label 'entrepreneurship' should be applied only to those things which conform to that core definition. Often the view's proponents argue that their view or definition should prevail and that those things which do not conform to it should be excluded. The basis for this 'core' view of entrepreneurship could be a belief by many people that there is an identifiable and distinct core behaviour which can be recognised when it is seen and distinguished from other behaviours and which is accepted as entrepreneurship by most observers with little or no significant dispute or misperception. However, so far, there has been no significant agreement on a definition of 'core' entrepreneurship and a lack of suggestions of what those other things are if they are not entrepreneurship.

Explore

The third form of response is that given by those who want instead to retain a wider, all-embracing approach to entrepreneurship, apparently in the belief or hope that by continuing to engage in exploratory research the problem will eventually be resolved. For instance, Audretsch et al., in a paper on the 'Making Sense of the Elusive Paradigm of Entrepreneurship',[30] agree that entrepreneurship apparently means different things to different people and recognise that the term entrepreneurship is an elusive one. But they describe entrepreneurship as 'a phenomenon' in the singular, anticipate that 'future research will continue to expand the domain of entrepreneurship literature' and argue for an 'eclectic paradigm of entrepreneurship theories as a way forward through the apparent "jungle" of literature that exists today'. They note that, as described earlier, a response to the proliferation of interpretations of entrepreneurship has been to propose that the field should be narrower and more defined – thus in effect restricting it to a set of definitions which are mutually consistent – but they argue that any definition is a construct which can be used to build theories and guide research and so the wider approach should be retained.

A variation of this exploratory view of entrepreneurship is to recognise that, as result of this ongoing exploration of entrepreneurship and its outcomes, our concept of entrepreneurship has evolved and that entrepreneurship itself, at least in how the concept is applied and used, has been redefined and should change further. For instance, in 2015 in his address to the International Council for Small Business (ICSB) on becoming its president Kim put forward the view that the early application of entrepreneurship, or entrepreneurship 1.0 as he called it, 'was for individual problem solving, entrepreneurship 2.0 was for companies and organisations, but now entrepreneurship 3.0 is for societal problem solving'.[31]

Another possibility: entrepreneurship does not exist?

Thus the responses of these commentators to an apparent proliferation of different views are in some cases to ignore them, in some cases to seek to define at least a clear core meaning and in some cases to continue to explore in the expectation of eventually finding the yet-to-be-revealed underlying links which will resolve the differences. However, what all these responses have in common is that they still appear to maintain the underlying belief that entrepreneurship is fundamentally a single identifiable condition.

Nevertheless the reality seems to be that the search for entrepreneurship has produced many different perceptions of what entrepreneurs are and a variety of different definitions of entrepreneurship. Despite the different responses which seem to have been offered to this variety, this chapter suggests that the differences have not been resolved. Ignoring them does not resolve them, treating only some of them as the core view has not led to a satisfactory definition of this core view – or indicate what the non-core others are – and continuing to explore the area to try to find a satisfactory linking theory has not (yet?) produced results.

Therefore this book suggests that although (almost) all the explanations offered still appear to hold to the assumption that entrepreneurship is essentially a single discrete phenomenon, another possible explanation for the variety of observations is that this assumption is wrong and that entrepreneurship does not in reality exist as we have thus conceived it. This possibility is explored further therefore in the next chapter.

Notes

1 W. B. Gartner, '"Who Is an Entrepreneur?" Is the Wrong Question', *American Journal of Small Business*, Vol.12 No.4, 1988, pp. 11–32.

2 J. Harris and J. Deacon, 'The Operation and Meaning of a Language for Enterprise and Entrepreneurship in Research, Policy and Practice', paper presented at the *36th ISBE Conference*, Cardiff, November 2013.

3 The National Policy and Advisory Board for Enterprise, Trade, Science, Technology and Innovation, *Towards Developing an Entrepreneurship Policy for Ireland* (Dublin: Forfás, 2007), p. 24.

4 W. J. Baumol, R.E. Litan and C. J. Schramm, *Good Capitalism, Bad Capitalism, and the Economics of Growth and Prosperity* (New Haven: Yale University Press, 2007), p. 3.

5 Blurb from Edward Elgar for the book *Essentials of Entrepreneurship* (e-mail 8 Apr 2014).

6 W. J. Baumol, 'Entrepreneurship: Productive, Unproductive, and Destructive', *Journal of Political Economy*, Vol.98 No.5, pt.1, 1990, p. 897.

7 P. Drucker, *Innovation and Entrepreneurship* (Oxford: Butterworth-Heinemann, classic edn, 2007), p. 19.

8 J. J. Liptak, *Entrepreneurial Readiness Inventory* (St. Paul, MN: JUST Works, 2009), p. 1.

9 M. Henrekson, *Entrepreneurship, Innovation and Human Flourishing* (Stockholm: Research Institute of Industrial Economics, IFN Working Paper No.999, January 2014).

10 J. Keane, *The Life and Death of Democracy* (London: Simon & Schuster, 2010), p. 30.

11 L. Siedentop, *Inventing the Individual* (London: Penguin Books, 2015), p. 39.

12 D. Graeber, *Debt: The First 5,000 Years* (London: Melville House, 2014), p. 187.

13 P. Burns, *Entrepreneurship & Small Business* (Basingstoke: Palgrave Macmillan, 2011), p. 11.

14 J. Cornwall, *The Entrepreneurship Educator Newsletter*, May 2012, www.planningshop.com.

15 Reported in H. H. Stevenson, 'Intellectual Foundations of Entrepreneurship', in

H. P. Welsch (ed), *Entrepreneurship: The Way Ahead*, (New York and London: Routledge, 2004), p. 3.

16 A. A. Gibb, 'SME Policy, Academic Research and the Growth of Ignorance, Mythical Concepts, Myths, Assumptions, Rituals and Confusions', *International Small Business Journal*, Vol.18 No.3, 2000, p. 16.

17 The *Entrepreneurship and Education Action Plan*, published in March 2003, a joint plan developed by the Department of Enterprise Trade, and Investment (DETI, the Department of Education (DE) and the Department for Employment and Learning (DEL).

18 U. Hytti and P. Kuopusjärvi, 'Three Perspectives to Evaluating Entrepreneurship Education: Evaluators, Programme Promoters and Policy Makers', paper presented at the *efmd 34th EISB Conference*, Turku, 2004, based on *Evaluating and Measuring Entrepreneurship and Enterprise Education*, Small Business Institute, Turku, Finland, 2004 – from a Leonardo funded project.

19 W. J. Baumol, 1990, Op Cit, p. 897.

20 Ibid., p. 894.

21 M. B. Low and I. C. MacMillan, 'Entrepreneurship: Past Research and Future Challenges', *Journal of Management*, Vol.14 No.2, 1988, p. 141.

22 S. Shane, *A General Theory of Entrepreneurship* (Cheltenham: Edward Elgar, 2003), p. 4.

23 D. Jasinski, 'A New Approach to Integrated Entrepreneurship Education', paper presented at the *ICSB 48th World Conference*, Belfast, 2003.

24 U. Hytti and P. Kuopusjärvi, Op Cit.

25 A. L. Zacharakis, W. D. Bygrave and D. A. Shepherd, *Global Entrepreneurship Monitor United States of America 2000 Executive Report* (Kansas City, MO: Kauffman Centre for Entrepreneurial Leadership at the Ewing Marion Kauffmann Foundation, 2000), p. 5.

26 Invest Northern Ireland, *Corporate Plan 2008–2011*, www.investmi.com (accessed 11 February 2009), p. 5.

27 H. M. Gabr and A. Hoffmann, *A General Policy Framework for Entrepreneurship*, FORA (Copenhagen, Denmark: Ministry of Economic and Business Affairs' Division for Research and Analysis, April 2006).

28 Ibid.

29 S. Bridge, K. O'Neill and S. Cromie, *Understanding Enterprise, Entrepreneurship and Small Business* (Basingstoke: Palgrave Macmillan, 1998), p. 39.

30 D. B. Audretsch, D. F. Kuratko and A. N. Link, *Making Sense of the Elusive Paradigm of Entrepreneurship* (The University of North Carolina, Greensboro: Department of Economics Working Paper 15–04, April 2015).

31 K.-C. Kim, 'Greetings from the 2015–16 ICSB President, Dr Ki-Chan Kim', International Council for Small Business, www.icsb.org/about-icsb-2/presidents-greetings/ (accessed 14 June 2015).

5   Revisiting entrepreneurship

So far this book indicates that the search for entrepreneurship has taken place in the context of many different perceptions of what entrepreneurs are and has produced a variety of different definitions of entrepreneurship. Chapter 4 concludes that, although we might have assumed that entrepreneurship is essentially a single discrete phenomenon, a possible explanation for the variety of observations is that this assumption is wrong and that entrepreneurship as we have thus conceived it does not in reality exist. This chapter therefore revisits our concepts of entrepreneurship in the light of that conclusion.

Stages in our entrepreneurship thinking

As Chapter 3 indicates, the French word 'entrepreneur' was introduced to economic dialogue initially by Cantillon. This term was eventually taken up by English speakers who, apparently in the 1920s, also added the suffix '-ship' to create a label for a concept apparently about, around and/or encompassing the activity of entrepreneurs. That coinage seems to have been readily accepted as the early examples of its use appear to take the concept of 'entrepreneurship' for granted and do not apparently see a need either to define or to query it. An example is Cole who, in 1942, wrote about entrepreneurship as an area of research because, he suggested, it had been a significant feature in American economic history.[1]

Subsequently the continued and frequent use of the label 'entrepreneurship' appears to have encouraged and supported a belief that there was a reality behind the term, thus increasing its unquestioned acceptance. As a result later researchers appear to have accepted that entrepreneurship exists, not least because there is a label for it, and have made attempts to identify and define that supposed reality by observing it or at least finding evidence for it. In particular, as Chapter 1 suggests, the search for entrepreneurship in many countries took off in the 1980s, prompted largely by a desire for economic development and, in particular, more employment. In the apparent assumption that entrepreneurship was the condition which caused more entrepreneurs to emerge who would, in turn, start more businesses and employ more people, governments wanted more entrepreneurship – and allocated budgets accordingly.

Although this apparent evolution of the concept of entrepreneurship from being a label for what entrepreneurs do to being the subject of a search for its nature and mechanisms has not necessarily been straightforward or steady, nevertheless it might be helpful to think of it as having happened in five broad steps or stages:

1   *Entrepreneurs.* The first step was the observation of certain economic actors who, following the lead of Cantillon, have been labelled 'entrepreneurs'.
2   *Entrepreneurship.* Those observations of entrepreneurs then seems to have been followed by the invention of the word 'entrepreneurship' – possibly initially as no more than a way of referring to entrepreneurs doing what entrepreneurs do and creating new enterprises.[2]
3   *The key to growth.* However, entrepreneurs creating new enterprises came to be seen as a crucial source of economic growth and, as entrepreneurship came to be seen as the condition which generated such entrepreneurial activity, the third step was to identify entrepreneurship as the key factor needed for economic growth.
4   *Government interest.* Therefore, those who wanted more economic growth – especially governments and those influenced by their policies/budgets – wanted more entrepreneurship and therefore wanted to know more about what it is in order to discover how to get more of it.
5   *Looking for a model of it.* That led to the fifth stage in this thinking which has been a search for an understanding of the entrepreneurship that people seem to want – and in particular for a deterministic model that will enable us to predict what should be done to get more of it and, as a consequence, deliver more economic growth.

Evidence for the first four of these stages is largely to be found in Chapter 3 which, for instance, describes the observations that Cantillon and others made about entrepreneurs and then comments on the introduction of the word 'entrepreneur'. It also summarises the apparent reasons for government interest in entrepreneurship as a supposed key factor in economic and employment growth, not least because small businesses are supposed to create employment and entrepreneurship is supposed to lead to more small businesses.

That leaves the fifth stage and it is examined in this chapter. It starts by reviewing what we have done to explore entrepreneurship and the nature of our approach to the search and its apparent results, which have not been positive; it then considers the basis of our concept of entrepreneurship and why we might have been searching for something which, as the conclusion to Chapter 4 suggests, does not exist.

A 'scientific' approach?

As Step 3 earlier suggests, a major feature of the search for entrepreneurship appears to be a cause-and-effect assumption that entrepreneurship is the condition which somehow creates more entrepreneurs. The assumption of cause and effect is a common one: it implies that, if the right cause can be identified and applied, the desired effect should be sure to follow. It is an aspect of classical determinism which, to a considerable extent, is the legacy of scientists like Newton whose approach, it has been said, was to see God as a sort of cosmic watchmaker who created his world from machinery which operates in accordance with physical laws.[3] Therefore, if those laws could be identified, they could be used to predict how that machinery would perform – and even how it might be influenced.

Thus, with Newtonian thinking, scientific understanding moved forward by seeking to identify the rules which would enable people to predict the future from the present. Adam Smith was born a few years before Newton died, and it has been suggested that what he was trying to do when he wrote *The Wealth of Nations* was to establish the then-newfound discipline of economics as a science on the assumption that economies, too, would operate in accordance with such laws.[4] More recently similar thinking has been applied to entrepreneurship, and the assumption has apparently been made that if it is to be a discipline worthy of study, then it, too, should be shown to be deterministic. Bygrave, for instance, in 1989 commented that if entrepreneurship 'is to grow in stature as a separate discipline, it will need to develop its own distinct methods and theories'.[5]

Bygrave labelled entrepreneurship as a science, albeit an applied one, when he described it as 'one of the youngest paradigms in the management sciences' which had 'emerged by using the methods and theories of other sciences'.[6] He also suggested that many such applied sciences suffered from 'physics envy' because it was such a deterministic science and that entrepreneurship researchers were no exception. However, as he pointed out, Schumpeter introduced the modern concept of the entrepreneur at about the same time Rutherford introduced the modern concept of the atomic nucleus. But whereas physicists since then have done much to explain the structure of the nucleus, we still can't agree on a definition of the entrepreneur.[7]

Box 5.1   Clocks and clouds

In his book, *The Social Animal*, Brooks[8] quotes Lehrer as noting that one of the great temptations of modern research is that it tries to pretend that every phenomenon is a clock, which can be evaluated using mechanical tools and regular techniques.

Lehrer borrows this analogy from Sir Karl Popper who compared clouds and clocks, suggesting that:

> My clouds are intended to represent physical systems which, like gases, are highly irregular, disorderly, and more or less unpredictable. I shall assume that we have before us a schema or arrangement in which a very disturbed or disorderly cloud is placed on the left. On the other extreme of our arrangement, on its right, we may place a very reliable pendulum clock, a precision clock, intended to represent physical systems which are regular, orderly, and highly predictable in their behaviour.[9]

According to Sir Karl, because Newton explained the motions of the planets in a very accurate and clock-like way, we have tended to think that fundamentally most things are clock-like and therefore, if we try hard enough, we will find a way of predicting their behaviour – but this is not the case and most things are clouds. In commenting on this, and echoing some of Sir Karl's conclusions, Lehrer noted that 'the mistake of modern science is to pretend that everything is a clock. . . . But that approach is doomed to failure. We live in a universe not of clocks but of clouds.'[10]

However, this fifth stage of entrepreneurship thinking seems to be a classic example of a clock-like approach (see Box 5.1). We have sought to identify the 'laws' to which entrepreneurship conforms in order to use them to predict entrepreneurial behaviour – as Newton developed his laws of mechanics and gravity, which enabled us then to predict the future motions of the planets apparently with clock-like precision. And we have hoped to be able to use such laws, not only passively to predict entrepreneurship, but also to understand how actively we might influence it and stimulate more of it.

Therefore, explanations or models of entrepreneurship have been sought which would predict or at least describe how it works. As Shane and

Venkataraman declare in their paper on the promise of entrepreneurship as a field for research:

> For a field of social science to have usefulness, it must have a conceptual framework that explains and predicts a set of empirical phenomena not explained or predicted by conceptual frameworks already in existence in other fields.[11]

However, at the end of their paper, Shane and Venkataraman acknowledge that 'many skeptics claim that the creation of such a body of theory [for entrepreneurship] and the subsequent assembly of empirical support for it are impossible', but they add that they hope that other scholars will join their efforts 'to prove those skeptics wrong'.

The search for entrepreneurship

But have those other scholars been effective in their efforts? The earlier arguments support the view, introduced in Chapter 1, that the search for entrepreneurship would appear to have been strongly influenced by two key assumptions:

- The assumption that entrepreneurship exists as a specific, discrete, identifiable phenomenon which somehow produces more and/or better entrepreneurs.
- The assumption that this phenomenon which we call entrepreneurship is deterministic in that it operates in a consistent way in accordance with 'rules' which can be identified and from which its behaviour can then be predicted.

Although these assumptions may be wishful thinking and may not be clearly and overtly stated or consciously shared by everyone, nevertheless they explain why entrepreneurship is of such interest, especially in government circles where there is a desire for more of the outcomes that entrepreneurship is supposed to produce. Therefore, it is further suggested that a significant objective in the search for entrepreneurship has been to try to identify the 'rules' indicated in the second assumption. Finding those rules and using them to construct a model of how entrepreneurship works would not only help to show governments how to promote more entrepreneurship, but would also prove the correctness of the assumptions themselves.

At one time McClelland suggested that he had found such a model. As indicated in Chapter 3, he set out to explore the hypothesis that 'achievement motivation is in part responsible for economic growth'[12] and refined this to 'the hypothesis . . . that a society with a generally high level of *n* Achievement will produce more energetic entrepreneurs who, in turn, produce more rapid economic development'.[13] Therefore he made suggestions for increasing levels of *n* Achievement. However, although McClelland suggested there was empirical evidence for his theory, subsequent scrutiny of this idea appears to have found serious flaws,[14] and although some still maintain that entrepreneurs have a high need for achievement, increasing the level of that need is not now seen as a deterministic way of creating more entrepreneurs.

One of those who have discounted McClelland's ideas was Kilby who, as early as 1971 in his book on *Entrepreneurship and Economic Development*, considered seven 'theories of entrepreneurial supply', including McClelland's theory – but he concluded that 'none of [them] can be judged to achieve an acceptable level of empirical verification'.[15] More recently Shane also attempted to find a framework for entrepreneurship. As he sees it: 'almost every explanation of business and, for that matter, capitalism itself, relies on entrepreneurship as a corner stone'[16] and therefore, given the level of interest devoted to it, 'one would think that researchers would have deep insights into understanding this phenomenon'.[17] Consequently, because he claimed that 'scholarly understanding of this field is actually quite limited',[18] he attempted 'to offer an overarching conceptual framework'.[19] However, although he produced a book entitled *A General Theory of Entrepreneurship*, in it he admitted that development of the theory was still at an early stage and the evidence for it was limited.[20]

The results of the search

The search for entrepreneurship does appear to have been the result of stage four of the thinking model suggested at the beginning of this chapter, and almost all the commentators mentioned here would seem to fit into stage five in that they are either trying to find, or at least are describing attempts by others to identify, predictive explanations of entrepreneurship. However, it is a conclusion of this book that all those attempts have failed. Despite, as Shane indicates, the need for it, and despite the searches, so far a successful deterministic theory of entrepreneurship does not seem to have been produced. Although Shane hoped that further work would refine his theory, it would seem that that has not happened and that his and other ideas have not led to a predictive theory. It was over 25 years ago that Bygrave commented that 'in contrast with physics, entrepreneurship has no great theories',[21] and it would seem that his observation still holds.

It was suggested earlier that the search for entrepreneurship would appear to have been strongly influenced by two key assumptions: that entrepreneurship exists as a specific, discrete, identifiable phenomenon which somehow produces more and/or better entrepreneurs and that the phenomenon which we call entrepreneurship is deterministic in that it operates in a consistent way in accordance with 'rules' which can be identified and used to predict its behaviour. However, Chapter 4 suggests that the first of those assumptions may be false, as there is still a multiplicity of different definitions of entrepreneurship, and this chapter suggests that that second assumption also fails in so far as the projected deterministic condition has not been satisfactorily identified.

These findings, this chapter concludes, are further indications that the search for entrepreneurship has not been productive. Not only has it not produced a single accepted definition of what constitutes entrepreneurial activity – never mind a practical theory about what causes or stimulates entrepreneurship – but also many of the descriptions and definitions of entrepreneurship that have been offered do not attempt to be predictive and refer only to the activity of supposed entrepreneurs, not to what might cause that activity. Could it be, therefore, that the different observations of entrepreneurship are, in the terms of Box 5.2, observations of artichokes not of an elephant? This suggests that, despite a clear desire for an explanatory description, in practice the word entrepreneurship reflects only varieties of effects or states of being and not a cause of such effects – that it refers only to people acting entrepreneurially and not to something that might lead them to act in that way. And, as they act entrepreneurially in a range of different ways, there are a range of different descriptions or definitions of entrepreneurship.

Box 5.2   Elephants or artichokes?

There is a story of three people who were blindfolded and then each asked to feel an object and say what they thought it was. It was actually an elephant, but the person who felt its trunk identified it as a hose, the one who felt the tail identified it as a brush and the third who felt a leg identified it as tree. Nevertheless, despite their having been identified as different things, they were all related parts of the same object. Further, once it is clear that they are all parts of an elephant, then how each part will behave can be predicted from an understanding of elephants and how they move and operate.

But what about artichokes? Apparently on the basis of taste, globe artichokes, Jerusalem artichokes and Chinese artichokes are all called artichokes – although the bits that are eaten are the base of the flower bud of a globe artichoke, the tubers growing on the roots of a Jerusalem artichoke or the tuberous underground stems of a Chinese artichoke. Despite the similarity in taste, they are not related. Globe artichokes are a variety of thistle, Jerusalem artichokes are related to sunflowers (and are called 'Jerusalem' supposedly as a corruption of 'girasole' – the Italian word for sunflower) and Chinese artichokes are a perennial herb of the mint family. Tasting the same and being called artichokes does not make them the same thing.

Which analogy best fits our perceptions of entrepreneurship? Although people may perceive it in different ways, does entrepreneurship nevertheless exist as a single, objectively distinguishable behaviour – or are the things to which different people apply the label 'entrepreneurship' sometimes different activities, albeit with some similar aspects, to which people have been accustomed to give the same label? If it is the latter, then trying to agree on or impose a single definition of entrepreneurship will not be productive and continuing to insist that entrepreneurship as variously defined is all the same thing will be counterproductive.

A predisposition to expect a theory?

It was suggested earlier that the search for a predictive theory of entrepreneurship has been driven both by a desire for such a theory in order to be able to present entrepreneurship as a legitimate and useful scientific subject for study and by a wish for a theory which would explain entrepreneurship and indicate how more of it could be developed. Is there, however, another reason for expecting to find such a theory because of the word 'entrepreneurship' itself?

Porter's cluster theory has recently been very influential in economic policy circles, but a paper on 'deconstructing clusters' suggests that Porter's clusters are constructs which are 'as much analytical creations as they are objectively real phenomena' and which 'have no essential self-defining boundaries, whether in terms of inter-sectoral or inter-firm linkages, information networks, or geographical reach'.[22] Could the same be said of entrepreneurship – that it, too, is a construct with no essential self-defining boundaries? Pursuing a similar theme Moroz and Hindle consider the question of whether entrepreneurship is genuinely distinct from any other well-studied phenomenon. They suggest that answering this involves trying to establish 'what *always* happens in every set of activities classifiable as constituting an "entrepreneurial" process that *never* happens in any other type of process' in order to show that entrepreneurship 'involves a process that has at its core something simultaneously generic and distinct'. They examine thirty-two 'models of entrepreneurial process' but, although they do not dismiss the concept of entrepreneurship as a distinct phenomenon, they find that the models are 'highly fragmented in their claims' and insufficient as a basis for establishing an understanding. Therefore they suggest that without greater clarity and agreement 'it is a delusion to think that entrepreneurship qualifies as a research field with genuine philosophical integrity'.[23]

'Entrepreneurship' is 'entrepreneur' with the suffix '-ship' added – and is it that suffix which has encouraged us to go to stage five in our thinking? Is entrepreneurship, for instance, like leadership? One definition of leadership is that it is 'exercising such an influence upon others that they tend to act in concert towards achieving a goal which they might not have achieved so readily had they been left to their own devices'[24] – and there does appear to be something that can be taught which will enable people to do that. Thus there does appear to be a common condition among leaders which can be influenced – as the suffix '-ship' in leadership indicates.

But can we say the same about runners? Box 5.3 describes the invented concept of 'runnership' as the linking condition between people who run and therefore the state of being that makes them want to run. However, it is suggested that in practice the idea of runnership would be misleading because people clearly run for a wide variety of different reasons and there is nothing they all have in common which would let us in each case predict in advance who will run. Although some people may be identified as likely to run because of their occupation or declared intent, many runners can only be identified as such retrospectively after they have been observed to run. Further, simply as a label for the act of running, the term runnership is not needed because we already have the word 'running'. Is it the case that 'runnership' doesn't exist as a useful word/concept because, although we have 'runners' (stage one thinking), there doesn't appear to be anything more?

Box 5.3   'Runnership'?

Human beings, when they move upright on their legs, can either walk or run. We can clearly and objectively define running and distinguish it from walking, and we note that, although often people walk, sometimes some of them prefer to run. But why do they do that instead of walking, and could we use the term 'runnership' to describe this condition? What then would runnership be? Would it just be an acknowledgement that sometimes some people run – or could it be the condition which causes them to run or explains why they run?

Why do people run? A sprinter might run to win a medal, a commuter might run to catch a train, a football player might run to score a goal, a jogger might run to keep fit, a cricketer might run because that is the activity which generates a score and a thief might run to escape arrest after committing a crime. We can objectively determine that what they are doing is running and therefore we could refer to them all as 'runners'. But if we labelled them all as runners, would we start to think that they had something in common beyond just on occasion having run? If we were to call their activity 'runnership', would that suggest that it was an identifiable condition? We might observe a fitness enthusiast running to get some exercise, a traveller running to catch a bus, a lepidopterist running to catch a butterfly or a tennis player running to return a ball – but is it credible to think that there is some quality they all share which would allow us to predict that they will run? Of course they would have the act of running on at least one occasion in common, but would a label such as 'runnership' lead us to think that there was something more? And in particular would identifying them all as runners lead us to think that they could be identified as such before they are observed in the act of running?

Suppose we wanted more people to run and those who do run to do it more and/or better. Is there anything that would persuade more people to run and encourage all of the different types of runners to improve their running – or would we have to treat each category of running separately? And would we actually want to persuade all those categories of runners to run better? Clearly many of us would like to encourage 'our' athletes to run better and win more medals – but what about the commuters and especially the criminals? Do we want the latter to be better at escaping from arrest?

Is the reality not only that we don't necessarily want them all to run better, but also that there is nothing that they all share which will identify them as people who are going to run? Ought we to accept that, although we might expect that some of them will run – for instance, because of their occupations – there is no objectively identifiable quality they all have which will allow us to identify them before they run, or a single factor or group of factors which will influence how well each of them runs? One condition can't explain all the instances of running in a way which will help us not only to predict when such people will run but also help us, if we want more running, to create triggers to get it to happen more. So surely labelling them as runners

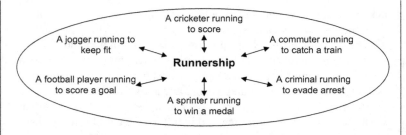

Figure 5.1 Instances of 'runnership'

and calling their condition 'runnership' would tell us nothing extra and be of no use in making predictions about running.

We could draw a diagram like Figure 5.1 which suggests that 'runnership' is the common connection between the various different instances or categories of running. But would 'runnership' then exist in reality just because we have suggested it in a diagram? What really is in the central area to which we have applied that label? Runners are runners because they all run – but that is the only thing they all have in common. They do not all run for the same reasons or for predictable reasons and/or respond to the same incentives to run; they do not all run to the same extent; they do not all want to improve their ability to run; they do not all enjoy or relish running; they do not all plan in advance to run; and they do not all see themselves as runners and thus as having anything in common with the other runners.

So if some runners have something in common, such as running being an essential part of their sport, and if we wanted to improve the running ability of those sporting runners, we should concentrate on them and not the others. Calling the condition of all runners 'runnership' tells us nothing more about those people, and 'runnership' is not a scientific paradigm because it does not seek determinism – not least because of a recognition that there are no laws/rules about running which can be used to explain running when it happens and to predict when it will happen. Of course, some cases of running may be predictable – for instance, it might be predicted that Olympic sprinters will run in Olympic Games – but that only applies to Olympic runners, and it is predictable because they are Olympic athletes, not because they happen to run.

Therefore, we don't see the need for a concept of 'runnership' to explain their actions – and we don't think that there is a set of actions we could take to get all of them to do it more. Thus, although running is objectively distinct from walking, we realise that labelling people as runners adds no extra understanding, and we haven't felt a need to postulate the concept of 'runnership' because it is of no use.

Is it the case that, because it ends in '-ing', we expect the term running to refer to an activity and not necessarily to anything which might cause or trigger such activity but, because it ends in '-ship' we have expected 'entrepreneurship' to be something more? Is the reality that the concept of entrepreneurship is actually no more valid or useful than that of 'runnership' but the suffix '-ship' subconsciously suggests a condition like leadership? Therefore, has the act of attaching '-ship' to 'entrepreneur' encouraged us to think of entrepreneurship as something which, like leadership, we can encourage and/or facilitate, which we can predict will, in turn, lead to improved performance by those thus affected? If, instead, we just referred to people 'entrepreneuring' or acting entrepreneurially, would we think about them in the same way?

But, because we now have an accepted word for it, have we come to believe that there is a thing called entrepreneurship which links people who we identify as entrepreneurs (even though we can't yet clearly and objectively define entrepreneurs) and even leads them to act in that way? If entrepreneurship is not a deterministic condition which can be modelled to predict how and/or when it will occur – and such a condition has yet to be identified – then is it just a label for what entrepreneurs do when they do it? In that case is the '-ship' misleading and would the term 'entrepreneuring' serve us much better? Running is what people who happen to run do when they run. Is entrepreneurship/entrepreneuring no more than a label for what people do when we think they are being entrepreneurial – however we define that?

Over 30 years ago Martin said something similar about the activity of entrepreneurs when he commented that 'the entrepreneur is not identified by formal rank or title but retrospectively, after the successful act of innovation'.[25] Unlike being an entrepreneur, we can at least objectively define running, but one of the reasons that 'runnership' is not a helpful concept is that it does not help us to predict running, and in many cases we can only identify runners retrospectively.

Nevertheless do we cling to the concept of entrepreneurship, not just as a label for or a description of any entrepreneurial activity, but also as an explanation for it? But we have not managed to isolate and even objectively define such a factor and therefore, although there are those who will want

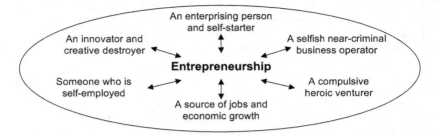

Figure 5.2 Instances of entrepreneurship

to continue the search for the underlying link, has the time come to try the alternative approach of abandoning the assumption that entrepreneurship as it has been variously conceived is not a single coherent phenomenon?

We appear to have developed the concept of entrepreneurship as the condition shared by all entrepreneurs (as suggested by Figure 5.2) and as elements of leadership shared by all successful leaders. Further, have we also assumed that, if we then discover how it works, that will enable us to predict when it will occur and to use that understanding to produce more entrepreneurs? But have we developed the concept of entrepreneurship because it is something which we have observed in reality – or have we conceived of entrepreneurship because we want there to be such a condition and because we can draw diagrams like Figure 5.2? And then, having conceived of it, have we then started to think of it as something that does really exist? Does Figure 5.2 really have any more validity than Figure 5.1? As one commentator said about theoretical concepts like this:

> Such imaginary constructs are of course what scientists refer to as 'models', and there's nothing intrinsically wrong with them. Actually I think a fair case can be made that we cannot think without them. The problem with such models . . . is that, once created, we have a tendency to treat them as objective realities.[26]

'Economics', it has been said, 'is not a science like physics or chemistry, but a political exercise'.[27] Could the same be said of entrepreneurship? Has the time come to abandon the scientifically inspired concept of entrepreneurship as a single, real, homogeneous, objective and deterministic condition and see what that change of perception might do for our understanding of some of the occurrences, effects or conditions which we have variously labelled 'entrepreneurship'? Should we re-label the activity we see as entrepreneurial activity or 'entrepreneuring' and reassess it on that basis?

Reflections on 'entrepreneurship'

The evidence reviewed earlier suggests that we can neither define entrepreneurship nor model it. Indeed it might be argued that, if we can't define entrepreneurship, how could we hope to model it or, conversely, if we can't model it, might that may be because it is not a single clear deterministic factor and we shouldn't expect to be able to define it as such?

Therefore, instead of looking for a connecting link between the different interpretations of entrepreneurship, and even assuming that such a link would help to explain why entrepreneurship occurs, should we cease to think of entrepreneurship as a single connected phenomenon? As far back as 1985 Gartner reported that a review of the entrepreneurship literature suggested that differences among entrepreneurs were as great as differences between entrepreneurs and non-entrepreneurs and that 'it has been consistently pointed out . . . that variables that are assumed to differentiate entrepreneurs from non-entrepreneurs frequently do not bear up under close scrutiny'.[28] Therefore, instead of conceiving of entrepreneurship as the condition which unites and even causes entrepreneurial activity, should we recognise that it is no more than a label which we apply not very consistently to certain activities when they happen – and is therefore of little help in trying to predict or control them? This is not a new proposal. In 1988 Gartner also observed that 'the entrepreneur is not a fixed state of existence. Rather entrepreneurship is a role that individuals undertake to create organisations.'[29] And in 1990 Hornaday noted that the words entrepreneur and entrepreneurship continued 'to bedevil small business scholars' and suggested that they should be dropped as the concept of entrepreneurship was 'not helpful in small business research', as it was 'not appropriate for the study of small business owners'.[30] So has the time come to follow his advice?

In conclusion

It may not be necessary to see, hold and/or feel something to be sure that it exists. When the author was on safari in Africa he didn't actually see a leopard. One night the party heard one, the next morning they found what was left of a fresh kill and the guides pointed out fresh leopard droppings – so they saw plenty of indications that there was a leopard there. In general the guides were very keen to show what could be learnt from such signs, even if they didn't actually see the animals in question. That is how trackers work – they try to discover the whereabouts and activities of animals, or people, from the tracks and other signs their targets leave. Thus the author believed that the signs he saw did indeed indicate that he was in the presence of a leopard – but would he have said the same of the supposed signs of a yeti?

Nevertheless many people have a concept of a yeti of which some claim to have seen signs or even to have observed one directly – but it has not yet been shown scientifically to exist.

This book suggests that an examination of our search for entrepreneurship indicates that:

- We have wanted entrepreneurship as we have conceived it to exist and we have wanted there to be a discoverable and deterministic model which explains how and why it happens.
- Further we seem to have conflated the concept of entrepreneurship as the condition of being an entrepreneur with the concept that there is something that causes people to be entrepreneurs. Something may have that effect, but is it the same thing in every case – and is it known and controllable? This confusion is often not acknowledged or even recognised and may arise because of a physics-like assumption that discernible effects must have identifiable causes.
- However, we have not found a credible cause of entrepreneurial activity and we have not even been able to agree on a single clear identification of such activity. Instead there are varied, and even conflicting, ideas about who is an entrepreneur and what entrepreneurs are like.
- Thus, has the search for entrepreneurship actually produced more questions than answers – possibly because what has been sought for does not actually exist in the form supposed?

We have been assuming that entrepreneurship as we have conceived it does exist as an observable homogeneous condition which leads people affected by it to become entrepreneurs (and thus to start and/or grow businesses). We may not know precisely what that condition is or how it works, but, because we believe that it exists, we haven't felt a need to speculate too much, as we expect that we will eventually corner and capture it and that we will then be able to examine it and thus learn more about it. But those are only assumptions and, if they are wrong, what other assumptions should now be questioned because they have been built upon those questionable foundations? Over 40 years ago Kilby[31] likened the search for the source of entrepreneurship to hunting the 'Heffalump': the much sought after, but never quite found, animal in *Winnie-the-Pooh*, although even he hedged his bets and also suggested that with a better trap and by looking in a different area, future hunters might still capture it. Has the time come to take Kilby's Heffalump analogy at face value and accept that our quarry only exists in our imagination?

If entrepreneurship does not exist as one clear thing, what would be the implications of changing our views about it? What are the blinkers which the assumption of the unity of entrepreneurship has applied? Would it be better instead to assume that what we had labelled as entrepreneurship is probably several different things and that what applies to one does not necessarily apply to another? These, and other possible consequences, are considered in the following chapters.

Notes

1 A. H. Cole, 'Entrepreneurship as an Area of Research', *The Journal of Economic History*, Vol.2 supplement, 1942, pp. 118–126.
2 M. B. Low and I. C. MacMillan, 'Entrepreneurship: Past Research and Future Challenges', *Journal of Management*, Vol.14 No.2, 1988, p. 141.
3 W. Bygrave, 'The Entrepreneurship Paradigm (I): A Philosophical Look at Its Methodologies', *Entrepreneurship: Theory and Practice*, Vol.14 No.1, 1989, p. 11.
4 D. Graeber, *Debt* (London: Melville House, 2014), p. 44.
5 W. Bygrave, Op Cit, p. 7.
6 Ibid.
7 Ibid., p. 14.
8 D. Brooks, *The Social Animal* (London: Short Books, 2011), pp. 166–167.
9 K. Popper, 'Of Clouds and Clocks – An Approach to the Problem of Rationality and the Freedom of Man', in *Objective Knowledge: An Evolutionary Approach* (1973).
10 J. Lehrer, 'Breaking Things Down to Particles Blinds Scientists to Big Picture', *Wired*, May 2010.
11 S. Shane and S. Venkataraman, 'The Promise of Entrepreneurship as a Field of Research', *Academy of Management Review*, Vol.25 No.1, 2000, pp. 217–226.
12 D. C. McClelland, *The Achieving Society* (Princeton, NJ: D. Van Nostrand Company Inc., 1961), p. 36.
13 Ibid., p. 205.
14 W. Bygrave, Op Cit, p. 13.
15 P. Kilby, *Entrepreneurship and Economic Development* (New York: The Free Press, 1971), p. 19.
16 S. Shane, *A General Theory of Entrepreneurship* (Cheltenham: Edward Elgar, 2003), p. 1.
17 Ibid.
18 Ibid., p. 2.
19 Ibid., p. 4.
20 Ibid., p. 270.
21 W. Bygrave, Op Cit, p. 13.
22 R. Martin and P. Sunley, 'Deconstructing Clusters: Chaotic Concept or Policy Panacea?', *Journal of Economic Geography*, Vol.3 No.1, 2003, pp. 13–14.
23 P. W. Moroz and K. Hindle, 'Entrepreneurship as a Process: Toward Multiple Perspectives', *Entrepreneurship Theory and Practice*, Vol.36 No.4, 2012, pp. 781–817.
24 N. F. Dixon, *On the Psychology of Military Incompetence* (London: Jonathan Cape, 1976), p. 214.
25 A. Martin, 'Additional aspects of entrepreneurial history', in C. A. Kent, D. L. Sexton and K. H. Vesper (eds), *Encyclopedia of Entrepreneurship* (Eaglewood Cliffs, NJ: Prentice Hall, 1982), p. 16.

26 D. Graeber, Op Cit, p. 354.
27 J.-H. Chang, *23 Things They Don't Tell You about Capitalism* (London: Penguin, 2011), p. 10.
28 W. B. Gartner, 'A Conceptual Framework for Describing the Phenomenon of New Venture Creation', *Academy of Management Review*, Vol.10 No.4, 1985, pp. 696–697.
29 W. B. Gartner, '"Who Is an Entrepreneur?" Is the Wrong Question', *American Journal of Small Business*, Vol.12 No.4, 1988, p. 28.
30 R. W. Hornaday, 'Dropping the E-Words from Small Business Research: An Alternative Typology', *Journal of Small Business Management*, Vol.28 No.4, 1990, pp. 22–23 and p. 25.
31 P. Kilby, Op Cit, p. 1.

6 Suppose entrepreneurship (as we have conceived it) doesn't exist

The earlier chapters suggest that the search for entrepreneurship has been based on the two assumptions that entrepreneurship exists as a specific, discrete, identifiable phenomenon which somehow produces more and/ or better entrepreneurs and that this phenomenon is deterministic in that it operates in a consistent way in accordance with 'rules' from which its behaviour can then be predicted. However, those earlier chapters also suggest that so far the search for entrepreneurship has revealed neither a clear, discrete phenomenon nor a practical deterministic model which could guide policy. This indicates that both assumptions may be wrong which in turn would lead to the conclusion that entrepreneurship, as we have conceived it, does not exist.

That conclusion may be simple to state, but what are its implications? Some, no doubt, will still insist there is a condition called entrepreneurship which affects some but not others and which can be recognised when it is seen – but attempts to identify its unique attributes/distinguishing features and/or its sources have so far been unproductive. Governments may continue to pursue it for its claimed economic benefits, not least because they have no alternative strategy – but again it is not possible to identify anything uniquely distinguishable which is being targeted by them and which does in reality deliver the benefits they seek. And others will no doubt still say that they dislike it and claim those who practise it are responsible for many of modern society's ills. But for all these people, entrepreneurship as they conceive it appears to be the encapsulation of their wishful thinking rather than the label for an objectively observed reality.

Therefore, the use of the word can be very confusing both because it can have many different meanings and because it has the suffix '-ship' which gives a false impression that the supposed condition must exist. Should we, therefore, stop using the word? What are the arguments for that and what might it mean for those who have been studying or seeking entrepreneurship? This chapter looks at these issues.

Should we stop using the word 'entrepreneurship'?

If, as this book suggests, entrepreneurship is not the homogeneous, distinguishable and deterministic condition that some appear to have assumed and the word is in practical reality no more than a label applied to a range of activities which we cannot consistently define, then what is the justification for using the word entrepreneurship rather than labels such as being entrepreneurial, entrepreneurial activity or 'entrepreneuring'? 'Entrepreneuring' might indeed be a better label for many of the activities that have been observed because it would not imply that it is any more than just an activity label and therefore would not suggest any element of determinism. Should we therefore make a conscious and deliberate decision to stop using the word 'entrepreneurship'?

Why should we abandon this word?

- The word 'entrepreneurship' is confusing because it can have different and sometimes conflicting meanings or associations. That leads to problems, for instance, when different sides of a discussion or debate assume different meanings – an example of which is that the different expectations and the requirements of funders, providers and/or consumers of entrepreneurship education can go unrecognised and therefore not addressed.[1]
- Even if the possibility of different meanings is acknowledged, the use of the same term can nevertheless lead to false parallels being drawn. An example of this, also from the field of entrepreneurship education, is that even when it is acknowledged that entrepreneurship as 'enterprise-for-new-venture-creation' courses differ from entrepreneurship as 'enterprise-for-life' courses, it sometimes appears to be assumed that they have sufficient in common to use the same course content.[2] Therefore, because a business plan–based syllabus is often already available for the former, it is frequently also used for the latter – whereas it is arguable that it is not even appropriate for the former,[3] and the latter, most would agree, needs a very different approach.
- Because the word carries the suffix '-ship', it will continue to lead to an expectation that it is more than just a label for an activity and instead indicates a deterministic condition.
- If we did stop using the word, we would have to find other words to use in its place. That might require more careful thought about the different meanings intended, so the alternative words chosen might then be more meaningful and so less confusing.

What else could we do? Are there satisfactory alternatives to dropping the word? In practice there appear to be two other possible courses of action:

- We could do nothing and just continue to use the word 'entrepreneurship'. That might be the easiest (laziest?) option to choose; however, it would mean ignoring the problems caused by using the word, so, although this might be the most likely course for many, it would just perpetuate the confusion.
- We could try to redefine entrepreneurship. Instead of just dropping the word, we could more carefully (re)define it and try to restrict its use only to that definition. But would such a definition have sufficient critical mass of acceptance to be effective – and so long as it still had the suffix '-ship' would it continue to suggest a deterministic condition which doesn't exist? Even if the word was redefined, the former use would still be there in old literature, and it is very likely many people would continue to use it for at least for some time in the old ways, so confusion would still reign.

Is dropping it a viable option? Is it practical to advocate not using it, especially as it is so deeply entrenched in academic circles, wider society and popular culture? It is suggested here that, unlike the case with trying to introduce a new standard definition, not using it does not have to be all or nothing. The decision whether to use it or not can be made by individuals and anyone who didn't use it, even if there are not many of them, would nevertheless help to improve their own thinking and to reduce future confusion from their own contributions. Even some reduction in its use would be better than none.

That brief appreciation of the benefits and the options suggests that dropping the word entrepreneurship could be very beneficial, that there is no other practical way of reducing the confusion caused by its use and that dropping the word is a practical option to advocate. Asking people to stop using the word would therefore seem to be the best option to pursue.

What would that mean for those who have been seeking it?

For those who have been using the word entrepreneurship and searching for its meaning and/or causes, what might be the implication of dropping the word? They may have thought they were seeking entrepreneurship, but why were they seeking it? Dropping the word because entrepreneurship doesn't exist as they had conceived it could lead to a realisation that it was only a means to an end and raise the question of what actually was the end that was being sought. If so, then it might bring more clarity about the real purposes.

Seekers of understanding and knowledge

The early commentators on or searchers for aspects of entrepreneurship seem to have been seeking or trying to establish elements of understanding – in particular about aspects of economic activity. Cantillon, for instance, seems to have concluded from his observations that there are three types of economic actors – one of which he labelled 'the entrepreneur'. Say then took this identification of the entrepreneur a stage further and suggested that the label should be restricted to innovators, and Schumpeter observed that an inevitable outcome of entrepreneurial activity was creative destruction.

Thus it might be said that they, and others like them, were seeking knowledge about (some of) the component parts of an economy and how economic activity developed. Largely this has been done, and still is being done, in an academic context as part of the research mission of academia – but often funded by government budgets. And there are other researchers also who largely do contract research paid for by those same budgets. But, whoever they are, what they have generally been seeking is an understanding of aspects of the economic process and often the sources of growth.

Seekers of learning

The second academic mission is teaching and its expected consequential learning – which is also a way of passing on the knowledge gained from research. One relatively early field of interest in entrepreneurship was manifest in what is often referred to as entrepreneurship education. It was in the late 1940s that Harvard Business School introduced its first entrepreneurship course, and it has been claimed that deliberate entrepreneurship education started as early as 1938 in Japan.[4] However, it is in the last 30 years or so that entrepreneurship education has become particularly popular. For instance in 2002 Robinson and Hayes conducted a survey of all 232 US universities with at least 10,000 students. Of these 215 (93 per cent) responded and of them 176 (82 per cent) offered undergraduate entrepreneurship courses. Ten years later Rae et al. surveyed HEIs in England and their report indicated that, of the 126 they had tried to survey, 116 (92 per cent) had responded of which 93 per cent reported that they supported student enterprise and graduate entrepreneurship – a response which indicates that it was available in at least 85 per cent of the whole sample.[5]

What is this education?

Traditionally, as indicated earlier, universities and other higher levels of the education sector have been concerned with both teaching and research. However, the early entrepreneurship educators do not seem to have been (re)searching to establish what entrepreneurship was – instead they were teaching what they understood it to be and what people were wanting to learn. Then, when, as indicated earlier, more institutions also took it up, often they just followed what the others appeared to be doing. Thus, when researchers explored what entrepreneurship means in this context, they found different interpretations. For example, as indicated in Chapter 3, Gibb spoke of enterprise education as being either 'about' or 'for' entrepreneurship,[6] Hannon added 'through' entrepreneurship'[7] and Hytti and Kuopusjärvi observed similar distinctions in the different roles which might be assigned to 'entrepreneurship' education programmes depending on whether the aim was learning to understand entrepreneurship, learning to become an entrepreneur or learning to become entrepreneurial.[8]

Why has it been delivered?

Why is entrepreneurship education so prevalent and apparently so important? At least initially, it seems that entrepreneurship education was developed and delivered because it was felt to be a helpful offering to students, but it may now often be pursued because there is official encouragement, and therefore budgets, for it. According to one article the reason for its popularity is 'in a word – economics. It pays!'[9] And according to another:

> To a large extent, recent enterprise and entrepreneurship initiatives, wherever located in the curriculum, have been heavily dependent on public finance. Educational enterprise and entrepreneurship policy makers have allocated and spent public money on the premise that enterprise and entrepreneurship education can make a difference to life chances and business opportunities.[10]

It is probably not coincidental that this expanded interest in entrepreneurship education developed at the time when, in many countries, universities were being encouraged, in addition to their teaching and research missions, to acknowledge a third mission which was concerned with the impact they have on societies and particularly on economies. Thus it has been suggested that, in many cases, the acceptance or adoption by HEIs of entrepreneurship and/or enterprise objectives has been motivated by a desire to access the third mission or 'third leg' stream of funding available to support it.[11]

Nevertheless there are other reasons for pursuing enterprise education, including employability: 'employability is high on the agenda of HEIs in the UK as well as in other developed nations' and 'there is a sound rationale for connecting enterprise and employability'.[12] However, it has also been suggested that the major motivation for many HEIs in engaging in enterprise education is that, in reality, they are just following the herd and 'operating in blind faith, following what other leading institutions do and through a desire or a need to be seen to be in alignment with new and changing central and regional government policy agendas [sic]'[13] or being 'unwilling to depart from perceived "good practice"'.[14]

Because of the source of much of this funding, a prime objective of enterprise education has often been to make a contribution to economic development – an impact which it was assumed would come from an increase in the number of entrepreneurs[15] who would in turn create more business start-ups[16] and in particular high-growth businesses[17] – and this assumption is accepted not least because it is government policy and a concept which is sometimes treated as being 'ostensibly beyond reasonable doubt or need for empirical validation'.[18] However, it has also been recognised that, because of this sort of thinking, 'there is a real danger that enterprise/entrepreneurship education comes to be perceived as a universal, all-embracing panacea that can address economic and societal structural inequalities'[19] – a view which assumes that all forms of entrepreneurship are essentially the same.

Seekers of economic growth

As indicated earlier much academic interest in entrepreneurship has been stimulated by the budgets available for exploring it – which have often come from governments interested in entrepreneurship because of its supposed impacts on their economies. Yet early commentators like Cantillon and Say do seem to have been seeking an explanation or an understanding of economic behaviour for its own sake and not, as far as can be seen, primarily because they were seeking a means to influence the behaviour of an economy. In contrast, whether directly or indirectly, a major factor in the recent searching for entrepreneurship education has been a belief that entrepreneurship contributes to economic development and/or growth. Therefore, it would seem that a desire for economic growth has also been behind much of the recent interest in this field.

A relatively early example of an entrepreneurship searcher stimulated by economic questions was the psychologist McClelland. As indicated in Chapters 3 and 5, the entrepreneur was not actually the prime focus of his interest and he was instead trying to explain economic growth. His main hypothesis, as expounded, for instance, in the new introduction to the 1976 edition of his book *The Achieving Society*, was that 'the need for Achievement is associated with more rapid rates of economic growth',[20] and he explained that the connection was that a society with a generally high need for Achievement (*n* Achievement) will produce more energetic entrepreneurs who will, in turn, produce more rapid economic development. Thus for him, the interest in the entrepreneur was as a means to the end of economic growth.

However, although *The Achieving Society* first came out in 1961, it was not for another 20 years or so that the economic growth aspect of entrepreneurs really started to attract attention – and that was after Birch's conclusions in 1979 that small businesses were the main source of net new jobs. Because many governments were looking for new jobs, they were then attracted to small businesses and interested in the factors that were supposed to lead to their creation. A key factor identified as supposedly leading to business creation was often initially labelled 'enterprise' – as seen, for example, in the UK in the 1980s when the Thatcher government declared its desire to inculcate an 'enterprise culture'; however, this later became conflated with and/or more often referred to as entrepreneurship. Thus enterprise/entrepreneurship was increasingly sought as a source, cause and/or trigger of economic growth and people (and particularly governments) wanted more of it. So they wanted to know what it was and what would influence it – but their purpose was to help them get more economic growth.

A recent example can be found in Denmark where, for some time, the Danish government has said that it has actively promoted entrepreneurship, and it has produced annual Entrepreneurship Index reports on entrepreneurship conditions in Denmark. It does this in the declared belief that 'entrepreneurship helps to create growth, both nationwide and regionally' and therefore 'the Government is keenly focused on entrepreneurship and growth in Denmark'.[21] According to the 2012 report the goals for these entrepreneurial activities are specified in terms of start-up rates for new enterprises and in particular the share of those start-ups which are high-growth enterprises.

In Ireland also entrepreneurship is believed to be important as 'a key element in the health and wellbeing of any thriving economy'.[22] Therefore the Irish government has issued a *National Policy Statement on Entrepreneurship in Ireland* which aims to identify clearly the framework needed to make Ireland one of the most entrepreneurial nations in the world. According to this statement 'it is vital that action is taken to optimise the role of entrepreneurship as an essential source of wealth creation and employment, thereby positioning it as a key element in the economic growth agenda'[23] and:

> We have to depend on our entrepreneurs to provide innovative products, processes and knowledge based solutions that will enable us to

preserve our hard earned progress, build our international reputation, improve our living standards and our employment creation.[24]

This belief in the efficacy of entrepreneurship for economic purposes seems therefore to amount to the assumptions that it is entrepreneurs who create and/or grow the businesses which in turn employ people and create wealth and growth – and that entrepreneurship is the condition which somehow leads to there being more entrepreneurs. Thus entrepreneurship been apparently increasingly viewed as the cause, source, trigger, key factor and/or missing ingredient required for economic growth.

However, as also indicated at the beginning of Chapter 7, so far attempts to deliver more jobs and/or economic growth by stimulating more entrepreneurship have failed, which might be expected once it is realised that entrepreneurship as thus conceived does not exist. So, if entrepreneurship doesn't exist, that raises fundamental questions such as what, if anything, does stimulate more entrepreneurial activity and/or more entrepreneurs and whether that does actually lead to more economic growth. These issues are therefore considered in Chapters 7 and 8.

Reflection

There can also be other categories of seekers after entrepreneurship – such as those who want to develop social entrepreneurship with the aim of trying to encourage more social entrepreneurs to create more social enterprises. When advocated by government departments, this is usually done in the apparent belief that social enterprises can solve a number of social problems. Others, however, may advocate social entrepreneurship because they think it will help grow the social economy which apparently for some is a preferred alternative to the supposed inefficiencies of public-sector provision, whereas others see it as better than the supposed excesses of private-sector enterprise.

In summary, therefore, it might be said that entrepreneurship is sought sometimes to benefit people and sometimes to benefit economies (which are in turn supposed to benefit people). But these benefits are sometimes sought in different ways. For instance, some of the benefits sought will come from an enterprise-for-life interpretation of entrepreneurship which, as Chapters 4 and 5 indicate, is a distinctly different thing from an enterprise-for-new-venture-creation approach. However, as earlier chapters show, the major impetus in the search for entrepreneurship has come from those who seek economic benefits, and in particular employment and/or growth, which they assume will flow from the enterprise-for-new-venture-creation form of entrepreneurship.

Although many people have used the word entrepreneurship apparently assuming it to be a single condition, Chapter 4 indicates that entrepreneurship has been interpreted in many different ways, and this chapter indicated that those seeking it have actually been looking for a variety of different things. Therefore, the use of the word has been confusing, and by finding replacements for it the different meanings and purposes are much more likely to be revealed. In this it may be rather like the development of medical knowledge (see also Box 4.3) when, at one time, the different possible causes of illness, such as infections of various forms, diet deficiencies, hereditary conditions or poisons were not appreciated. Instead, all illnesses were thought to be varieties of the same condition of dis-ease (disease) and, as a result, the different causes were not explored and different remedies were not sought. If, like disease, entrepreneurship is not the single condition we have assumed it to be, but if both academic research into the nature of entrepreneurship and policy delivery using it as a vehicle have been based on that assumption, then it should not be surprising that, tied to such a millstone, neither has been productive. So let us instead stop using the word and see what we can learn without that handicap.

The use of the word entrepreneurship, it is suggested here, has encouraged us to think that it exists as a single condition which somehow in a predictable way leads more people to behave entrepreneurially. Therefore we have sought it but have not found it. Moreover, not only have we not found that condition, but also we have not even been able to agree on a common definition of it, or even of an entrepreneur. As a result our continuing use of the word leads to confusion, miscommunication and other problems directly attributable to its use. Because efforts to redefine it are unlikely to work, this chapter recommends that the word should be dropped from economic discourse.

Notes

1 S. Bridge, C. Hegarty and S. Porter, 'Rediscovering Enterprise: Developing Appropriate University Entrepreneurship Education', *Education + Training*, Vol.52 No.8/9, 2010, pp. 722–734.
2 S. Bridge and C. Hegarty, 'Reconceptualising Curriculum Design for Entrepreneurship in Higher Education', *AISHE-J*, Vol.8 No.1, Spring 2016, pp. 2411–2414.
3 S. Bridge and C. Hegarty, *Beyond the Business Plan* (Basingstoke: Palgrave Macmillan, 2013).
4 D. Hannon, 'Philosophies of Enterprise and Entrepreneurship Education and the Challenges for Higher Education in the UK', *International Journal of Entrepreneurship and Innovation*, Vol.6 No.2, 2005, p. 106.
5 D. Rae, L. Martin, V. Antcliff and P. Hannon P., 'Enterprise and Entrepreneurship in English Higher Education: 2010 and beyond', *Journal of Small Business and Enterprise Development*, Vol.19 No.3, 2012, pp. 380–401.

6 A. A. Gibb, 'The Enterprise Culture and Education: Understanding Enterprise Education and Its Links with Small Business, Entrepreneurship and Wider Educational Goals', *International Small Business Journal*, Vol.11 No.3, 1993, pp. 11–34.

7 D. Hannon, Op Cit, p. 108.

8 U. Hytti and P. Kuopusjärvi, 'Three Perspectives to Evaluating Entrepreneurship Education: Evaluators, Programme Promoters and Policy Makers', paper presented at the *efmd 34th EISB Conference*, Turku, 2004, based on *Evaluating and Measuring Entrepreneurship and Enterprise Education*, Small Business Institute, Turku, Finland, 2004 – from a Leonardo funded project.

9 W. E. McMullan and W. A. Long, 'Entrepreneurship Education in the Nineties', *Journal of Business Venturing*, Vol.2, 1987, p. 263.

10 B. Jones and N. Iredale, 'Enterprise Education as Pedagogy', *Education + Training*, Vol.52 No.1, 2010, p. 14.

11 D. Hannon, Op Cit, p. 107.

12 D. Rae, 'Connecting Enterprise and Graduate Employability: Challenges to the Higher Education Culture and Curriculum?', *Education + Training*, Vol.49 No.8/9, 2007, p. 605.

13 D. Hannon, Op Cit, p. 107.

14 H. Matlay, 'Researching Entrepreneurship and Education, Part 2: What Is Entrepreneurship Education and Does It Matter?', *Education and Training*, Vol.48 No.8/9, 2006, p. 706.

15 L. W. Cox, S. L. Mueller and S. E. Moss, 'The Impact of Entrepreneurship Education on Entrepreneurial Self-Efficacy', *International Journal of Entrepreneurship Education*, Vol.1 No.2, 2002, pp. 229–245.

16 U. Hytti and C. O'Gorman, 'What Is "Enterprise Education"? An Analysis of the Objectives and Methods of Enterprise Education Programmes in Four *European* Countries', *Education + Training*, Vol.46 No.1, 2004.

17 L. Galloway and W. Brown, 'Entrepreneurship Education at University: A Driver in the Creation of High Growth Firms', *Education + Training*, Vol.44 No.8/9, 2002, pp. 398–405.

18 H. Matlay, 'Researching Entrepreneurship and Education, Part 1: What Is Entrepreneurship Education and Does It Matter?', *Education and Training*, Vol.47 No.8/9, 2005, p. 666.

19 B. Jones and N. Iredale, Op Cit, p. 14.

20 D. C. McClelland, *The Achieving Society* (New York: Irvington Publishers, 1976), p. A.

21 Danish Business Authority, *2012 Entrepreneurship Index* (Copenhagen: Danish Business Authority), www.erst.dk (accessed 17 January 2016), p. 5.

22 Department for Jobs, Enterprise, and Innovation, *National Policy Statement on Entrepreneurship in Ireland* (Dublin: Department for Jobs, Enterprise, and Innovation, 2014), p. 6.

23 Ibid., p. 55.

24 Ibid., p. 4.

7   What makes people more entrepreneurial?

(With a contribution from Spinder Dhaliwal)

One of the main reasons for searching for entrepreneurship has been that it was assumed to be a specific phenomenon which somehow produces more and/or better entrepreneurs who would start and/or grow more businesses. The search for entrepreneurship can be seen as a search for what makes people behave entrepreneurially – in effect a search for its source. Entrepreneurship policy is supposed to have been informed by the findings of that research but, as Bridge and O'Neill indicate, there seems to be little evidence that it has successfully achieved its aims anywhere and raised the level of entrepreneurial activity in a target group:

> It seems reasonable to conclude, from the evidence overall, that the methods so far applied have not worked in that they have not had the effect intended in improving rates of entrepreneurship.[1]

Here, then, is further evidence that the search for 'entrepreneurship' has not been productive and that a deterministic model does not exist to guide policy. But what, if anything, does encourage people to become productive entrepreneurs? Entrepreneurship may not be a valid concept, but entrepreneurs in various forms still exist and do still contribute to the economy and/or to society. So, even if our conceptions of entrepreneurship have not been helpful, we still want people who are enterprising and engage in entrepreneurial activity – and we have been trying to encourage that.

Knowing what hasn't worked can be a help in discovering what might work, so can we learn from our experience? This chapter considers where we have looked for the source of entrepreneurial activity, what those attempts might have in common and where else we might explore for a source of influence – if there is one.

Attempts to locate or use the source

In the search for the source of entrepreneurial activity, research has been carried out and theories have been advanced about the tendency of people to become entrepreneurs and/or behave entrepreneurially and what influences them. Supposedly based on such theories, policy has then attempted to influence people in order to encourage more entrepreneurial activity, and attempts have been made to assess the levels of such activity and the results of that policy. In order to do that, researchers, theorists, policy makers and statisticians have all had to make assumptions about where to apply their efforts. But what have those assumptions been and why have they been made?

Influential disciplines – and their application

In their book on *Exploring Entrepreneurship*,[2] Blundel and Lockett suggest that what they call entrepreneurship research has received significant overall contributions from five disciplinary perspectives: economics, psychology and behavioural studies, sociology, business history and political science. However, these perspectives have not all been equally concerned with the source of the supposed entrepreneurship:

- Economics, Blundel and Lockett suggest, may have the best claim to have invented 'entrepreneurship', but it could be argued that economists have tended just to assume that it exists without being too concerned about its sources and/or what has caused it to happen.
- Psychological and behavioural research is, according to Blundel and Lockett, a popular perspective because it relates directly to people's personal experience, and its application in this field includes the two broad strands of what makes people entrepreneurial and the behaviours associated with being entrepreneurial. This purports, therefore, in effect, to consider the sources of entrepreneurial behaviour, but its common theme is a focus on individual human beings where psychology appears to suggest a way of distinguishing entrepreneurs from non-entrepreneurs. Indeed, as Delmar and Witte[3] state in the introduction to a chapter on the psychology of the entrepreneur in another book: 'It is often believed that entrepreneurs are psychologically different from ordinary people.'
- Sociology (along with human geography and anthropology) does look beyond the individual and examines how entrepreneurship is shaped by larger, macro-level social forces such as gender or geographical effects.
- Business historians have tended to look at businesses and how they behave. Thus they often focus on the businesses as the main unit of analysis and do not ask too much about why people are entrepreneurs and start those businesses.

- Political science and, in particular, policy studies have on occasion considered the sources of entrepreneurial activity, not least because of a desire for policies which will promote and/or enhance it. However, they have often considered national (or regional) macro-level conditions – and policy has sought to address 'entrepreneurship' through macro-level schemes.

Therefore, overall, where a source or cause of entrepreneurial activity has been sought, the main effort has probably come from psychology with its focus on the individual. Some supporting effort has, however, also come from sociology and political science where the focus has often been on society at the macro level. Those disciplines have then, in turn, been used by researchers, theorists, commentators and others in a variety of different ways, as the following approaches show:

Traits – and the nature vs. nurture debate

Many of the attempts that have been made to explain why some people are more entrepreneurial than others and/or to predict who is most likely to be an entrepreneur have sought to establish whether this supposed entrepreneurship is the result of inherited characteristics (nature) or of upbringing or development influences (nurture). One 'nature' approach has sought to apply trait theory. Traits are presumed to derive from a person's genetic make-up, and attempts have been made to identify the particular traits, or combinations of traits, shown by people who are clearly entrepreneurs and then to assume that it is those traits which lead them to act entrepreneurially.

As suggested in Chapter 5, McClelland is a relatively early example of someone who thought he had found a model for entrepreneurial behaviour. He suggested that human motivation was underpinned by three dominant needs: a need for achievement, a need for power and a need for affiliation.[4] He further suggested that entrepreneurs in particular should have a high need for achievement (often referred to as *n* Achievement), and his results have been interpreted as suggesting that a high *n* Achievement would influence someone towards entrepreneurship.[5] As a result *n* Achievement (or sometime just *n* Ach) has been described as the most widely cited characteristic, or trait, of entrepreneurs.[6]

Other models

However, a problem with the trait approach is that some entrepreneurs do not seem to have all of the supposed entrepreneurial traits, and some people with all the traits do not seem to be entrepreneurial. Therefore, instead,

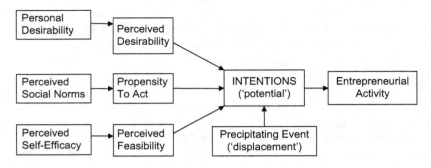

Figure 7.1 Krueger's intentions model of entrepreneurial potential (simplified)

Source: N. F. Krueger, *Prescription for Opportunity: How Communities Can Create Potential for Entrepreneurs* (Washington, DC: Small Business Foundation of America, Working Paper 93-03, 1995), p. 10.

cognitive models have been suggested which include a wider range of influences that might shape behaviour. An example is Krueger's approach (see Figure 7.1), which suggests a model of entrepreneurial potential based on factors which are thought to influence a person's intentions given the trigger of a suitable precipitating event.

A simpler model is implied in Shane's *A General Theory of Entrepreneurship* which suggests that entrepreneurship occurs when a prepared individual meets a suitable opportunity, and therefore Shane offers 'as a general framework for the field of entrepreneurship . . . the individual-opportunity nexus':

> The entrepreneurship process begins with the perception of [the] existence of opportunities, or situations in which resources can be recombined for potential profit. Alert individuals, called entrepreneurs, discover these opportunities and develop a product or service that will be provided to customers. These individuals then obtain resources, design organisations or other modes of opportunity exploitation, and develop a strategy to exploit the opportunity.[7]

Entrepreneurship policies and programmes

Policies and programmes designed to stimulate, encourage and/or support entrepreneurs and entrepreneurship generally are supposed to be evidence based, but often the evidence in question is not specified. Instead the assumptions behind policy in this area largely have to be deduced. For instance:

- So-called entrepreneurship education programmes seek to provide participants with the skills, understanding and/or attributes necessary to start businesses. They appear to be based on the assumption that providing these resources will encourage more entrepreneurial behaviour by the trainees – as if they either had not previously thought of doing it or a lack of such resources was holding them back.
- Start-up programmes often provide assistance such as guidance, training, finance and/or premises. They target individuals and require them to make application to the programmes, again with the objective of stimulating and/or enhancing individual business start-ups. Examples include grant and mentoring schemes which appear to assume that providing individuals with relevant resources will encourage entrepreneurial behaviour – also as if it was assumed that it was a lack of such resources which was preventing individuals from being more entrepreneurial.

Such policies are usually applied at a national or regional macro-level, and thus target everyone in a country or region or in a specific target section of the population, such as a gender or an age range. However, although they may target a wide number of people, they seek to address individuals and generally offer the sort of assistance which might help if the key requirement was to address the barriers presumed to be holding back those individuals.

Entrepreneurship surveys and statistics

Surveys and statistics are frequently called for to guide 'entrepreneurship' policy or to assess its effectiveness. They usually appear to assume that individual businesses are the key unit of analysis (not least because they are relatively easily counted and measured from existing accessible databases) or at least the individual people who might or do start businesses. For instance the Global Entrepreneurship Monitor (GEM) is one of the most widely used surveys in this field because it has sought to provide consistent inter-country (or inter-region) comparisons of the levels of entrepreneurship and the national (or sometimes regional) factors thought to influence this. Its main surveys, however, are of individuals, and it is these surveys from which GEM establishes the proportion of a national or regional population who are currently engaged in entrepreneurial activity (as GEM defines it).

The common feature(s)

To some it might appear to be obvious that it should be so, but what all these examples appear to have in common is that the focus has been on individuals – or on those macro-level conditions which are thought to affect individuals. It clearly seems to be assumed that that is where any impetus for entrepreneurial activity lies, but is that because it does indeed lie there, because it has (almost) always been assumed to lie there, or because that happens to be where it is most convenient to look (see Box 7.1) and/or because it is assumed that there is nowhere else it could be?

Box 7.1   The drunkard's search

There is a story about a policeman who saw a drunk man searching for something under a streetlight and asked what he was looking for. The man said he had lost his keys, and so they both looked under the streetlight together. When, after a while, they hadn't found the keys the policeman asked the drunk if he was sure he had lost them there, and the drunk replied 'no' and said he had lost them on the other side of the road. So the policeman asked why he was searching on this side, and the drunk replied, 'Because this is where the light is'.

This story may have given its name to what has been called the 'streetlight effect' – a type of observational bias where people only search for something where it is easiest and/or most familiar to look.

Alternative sources – where else might we look?

But if the source of entrepreneurial behaviour does not lie in the individual, where else might it be? Figure 7.2 is based on an interpretation by Cova and Cova and presents a diagram illustrating three levels at which it might be supposed human behaviour could be influenced and/or observed. However, it has been suggested that in Western societies the main emphasis has been either on the individual or on the macro-social level.[8] Thus key influences have been supposed to act on individuals, possibly aided or given effect by their genes, or to be due to issues affecting whole countries, regions or sections of society. Therefore, Cova and Cova suggest, the micro-social level of the tribe or social group has often been ignored.

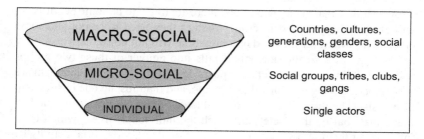

Figure 7.2 Levels of observation

Source: Based on B. Cova and V. Cova, 'Tribal marketing: the tribalisation of society and its impact on the conduct of marketing', *European Journal of Marketing*, Vol.36 No.5/6, 2002, p. 601.

As the previous section has shown, the search for entrepreneurship had largely conformed to the Covas's supposition about Western society thinking. It has been focussed mainly on individuals with occasional acknowledgement of supposed influences operating at the macro-social level, and it has rarely attempted to consider the micro-social level. Yet social influence, which mainly comes from micro-social–level contact, is very important in human society. Earls has explored this in his book, *Herd*, in which he states that we do what 'we do because of other people and what they seem to be doing',[9] and Rowson, in introducing a pamphlet based on the work of McGilchrist, a psychiatrist who has studied the two sides of the human brain, states that:

> The notion that we are rational individuals who respond to information by making decisions consciously, consistently and independently is, at best, a very partial account of who we are. A wide body of scientific knowledge is now telling us what many have long intuitively sensed – humans are a fundamentally social species, formed through and for social interaction.[10]

Given the indicated strength of the influence of this social interaction, it must be expected to affect many areas of human activity, not excluding enterprise. This social influence was clearly what Baumol[11] was referring to when he spoke of the strength of 'society's rules' which determined whether people who were entrepreneurial manifested this in productive, unproductive or destructive ways (see Box 3.1). Criminals often demonstrate a destructive, and illegal, form of entrepreneurship, and Ball's summary of the work of Campbell and Ormerod on criminality might be illuminating.[12] They postulate that in any population there are likely to be some people who will almost always resort to crime whether they need to or not and some others who, whatever the need or temptation, will not do so. However, they suggest, the bulk of the population falls into neither of these two groups and essentially does whatever their peers do. Thus, if those around them are seen to be engaging in crime, they will too, and if almost no one is, they will also desist. The result is that the overall level of crime is not determined by individuals but by the society in which the individuals live – which is an influence at the micro-social group level. Could entrepreneurial activity be somewhat similar with a few who will do it anyway, some who will never do it and a significant proportion who will, in essence, try to follow the herd and conform to the accepted norm of their social group?

Considering entrepreneurs from a social group perspective

There are examples of observations of levels of entrepreneurial activity which are consistent with a micro-social group level of influence. For instance Baumol's seminal work on productive, unproductive and destructive entrepreneurs[13] referred to earlier clearly highlights the critical influence of society's rules. 'Entrepreneurs', he suggests, 'are always with us' but 'how the entrepreneur acts at a given time and place depends heavily on the rules of the game'. Whether this entrepreneurial effort is allocated to productive, unproductive or destructive applications 'is heavily influenced by the relative payoffs society offers to such activities' – and that is often society acting at its most influential level which is the micro-social.

Another example can be found in the work of Ní Bhrádaigh who studied the historically disadvantaged and peripheral Gaeltacht community in Ireland.[14] Apparently this community had been accustomed to distrust entrepreneurs, but Ní Bhrádaigh notes that relatively recently the introduction of social enterprise seems to have paved the way for the subsequent evolution of for-profit entrepreneurs. A possible explanation for her finding is that, as Baumol describes in other situations, there may have been people in the community who displayed some entrepreneurial potential, but there is some anecdotal evidence that this was directed towards unproductive applications. If, in such circumstances, it was social disapproval which was acting as a disincentive for productive entrepreneurs, then possibly the social/community enterprise, by encouraging the community together to partake in productive enterprise, might have led to a form of 'tipping point' from which the members of the community could then start to see productive entrepreneurial activity as acceptable and even laudable, not just in the community as a whole but also in individuals.

This is also consistent with the work of Audretsch and Keilbach on what they have called entrepreneurship capital. In one study they looked at an analysis of the spatial distribution of entrepreneurial activity in Germany by plotting it at the level of the German Kreis (a unit of land division of which there are about 440 in Germany).[15] From this they concluded that 'entrepreneurship capital shows significant spatial autocorrelation and does spill over to neighbouring regions', and they took this 'as evidence that entrepreneurship capital is indeed linked to cultural variables that are strongly spatially clustered'. Could it be that the observation of this study was like that of Brownian motion in that, although it is not looking at the level of the relevant phenomenon, its focus is nevertheless at a level where the components are small enough to be influenced by variations in the phenomenon? In other words could the Kreis be areas which are small enough to show the variations of levels of encouragement in different micro-social groups? Could it also be that other entrepreneurial areas, such as Silicon Valley and the locations described by Florida,[16] also have a lot of entrepreneurs because of something in the nature of the societies and the social groups resident in those places?

Considering micro-social group influence doesn't mean that there are no individuals acting entrepreneurially in productive ways. Clearly there are, but if the focus is on the individual and on his or her personal attributes, then it is not immediately clear why those entrepreneurial individuals are found to be more heavily concentrated in some situations than in others. If, however, the focus is directed to the micro-social group, with its influence on the individuals within it, then that does provide an explanation for different concentrations of productive entrepreneurs.

Entrepreneurs in immigrant communities –
a relevant case study?

The prevalence or otherwise of entrepreneurs in immigrant communities (which is sometimes referred to by other terms such as ethnic minority entrepreneurship) is an aspect of entrepreneurial activity which provides a case study in which different perspectives can be considered. Archetypically immigrants are supposed to display high levels of entrepreneurial activity, but such high levels are not found in all immigrant communities. For instance Ram et al. in a discussion of 'ethnicity and entrepreneurship', refer to 'the apparent entrepreneurial flair of some ethnic groups, noticeably South Asians, and the below-average propensity for self-employment among other communities, in particular African-Caribbeans'.[17] Another contribution which acknowledges that entrepreneurial activity is not evenly distributed is a recent article by Carter et al. on barriers to ethnic minority and women's enterprise which indicates that it 'presents an overarching view of the evidence regarding enterprise diversity' and suggests that 'a noticeable feature of the enterprise policy discourse in the United Kingdom is the longstanding concern that entrepreneurial ambitions . . . are unevenly distributed across social groups'.[18]

However, in examining this, Carter et al. then consider the literature on ethnic minority–owned businesses and what it says about the barriers those businesses face in the areas of finance, markets and management – which are the factors traditionally thought to be influential. The article says little about the possible reasons why those people started businesses. It does refer to 'necessity entrepreneurship, emanating from labour market discrimination for example' but does not consider other potential reasons such as whether those communities view entrepreneurship with high regard. Thus, it looks at the businesses and the barriers which businesses are traditionally supposed to face, but it does not look at individuals and the social capital which their community encouragement might provide.

Many appear to have assumed that there is something about being an immigrant that means that entrepreneurial activity is generally high in all immigrant communities – but neither this assumption nor the 'necessity entrepreneurship' suggestion (as made, for example, by Carter et al.) indicates why entrepreneurs are prevalent in some immigrant communities but not in others. There is a relatively extensive literature on 'entrepreneurship' in immigrant and/or ethnic minority communities, but much of this has been aimed at defining and explaining differences between ethnic minority small firms and those of the general small business community.[19] When it comes to the source of this 'entrepreneurship', often the literature doesn't say much – and this may be more revealing than what it does say because what it does say often appears to be based primarily on a traditional perspective of what is supposed to influence entrepreneurs.

Nevertheless some authors do acknowledge a cultural influence, such as Dhaliwal, who suggests that:

> The creation of wealth is roundly applauded in the Asian culture. Temples, Gurdwaras (Sikh temples) and Mosques are richly decorated; the use of gold and precious gems in these places of worship is legendary. The communities are extremely generous and communal money has made many advances. This society equates wealth with success and it's nothing to be ashamed of. The basic driver is to succeed in life and dignity and respect are dependent on the ability to provide for the family. If you can help relatives and friends too, then your status is further enhanced. Wealth enables you to give.[20]

Such a societal attitude could help explain the higher levels of entrepreneurial activity apparently found in South Asian immigrant communities but not necessarily in African-Caribbean ones – and it is also consistent with the idea that the source of entrepreneurial activity is located in the communities themselves rather than just in some of their individual members.

It is therefore interesting that Ram et al. also indicate that, in the 21st century, there have been 'falling levels of self-employment among young UK-born Indians, coupled with evidence that many are using their high-level qualifications to enter professional careers'.[21] Indeed a member of the Indian community in the UK once commented to the author that his father had been an immigrant and a successful entrepreneur but, having absorbed the local culture and seen which occupations appeared to be most acceptable to the local establishment, he wanted his son to be a lawyer. Taken together these observations support the view that the stimulus of entrepreneurial activity among UK South Asians lies, not in individuals, but in their communities – and that community attitudes may change as the descendants of the original immigrants became more established in their new country.

Some reflections on micro-social group influence

How does the influence of micro-social groups operate – and can it easily be observed? Macro-social groups and individuals are relatively easy to identify and define, but micro-social groups are often less easy to delineate. Further people are often part of more than one such group – for instance, someone could mix with different groups drawn variously from family and friends, work colleagues, a golf club and/or a church. Also not everyone who is nominally a member of such a group will automatically be influenced by it, and different individuals are likely to be differently influenced, so they will not all react identically, and individuals may not even be conscious of any such influence. Therefore, surveying the separate effects of such groups is hard to do – but that does not mean that the influence is not real and strong. These observations taken from some research Earls did with 'drivers of the best-selling executive saloon in the UK, the BMW 3 series' illustrate the effects:

> Many of them look alike (as if there is an accepted and easily identified executive styling handbook): each professed their individuality but all of them used the same terms to do so and the same air of affected self-confidence. All of them commented on the excellence of the engineering and the uniqueness of the drive quality to justify their choice (so maybe advertising has contributed to the success of these run-of-the-mill bits of German engineering). And all of them admired each other's choice of transport and the uniqueness that it signified.[22]

		Institutional Support	
		Favourable	*Unfavourable*
Cultural Support	*Favourable*	Entrepreneurial	Repressed (bottom up)
	Unfavourable	Led (top down)	Stagnant

Figure 7.3 Institutional and cultural support

Source: Based on W. J. Dennis, 'Entrepreneurship, Small Business and Public Policy Levers', *Journal of Small Business Management*, Vol.49 No.1, 2011, pp. 92–106.

This emphasis on the influence of the social group is also consistent with Dennis's suggestion (see Figure 7.3) that, when it comes to policy efforts to influence 'entrepreneurship' and small business, institutional and cultural support act in different dimensions and, therefore, if cultural support is lacking, increasing institutional support will not compensate.[23]

Conclusion and implications

Box 7.2 A mushroom analogy

We can pull mushrooms up from a lawn as we can pull up daisy plant. But, although we will then have removed the source of the daisies, we will not have addressed the source of the mushrooms.

In seeking to discover why there are daisies growing in a lawn, it is necessary to understand that individual daisy plants grow from individual seeds and that each daisy grows where it does because that was where that seed happened to land. Some situations may be less suitable for daisies than others, and therefore a seed which lands on poor ground such as a gravel path, if it germinates, may not grow well – but that is due to the way in which each individual daisy plant interacts with its environment, and, although the ground may influence how the daisies in it grow, there is nothing in the ground which causes them to be there. The 'macro' condition of the lawn in terms of its nutrients, soil condition and drainage will affect all the daisies in it, but those daisies are not physically connected to each other so removing one will not directly affect the others but removing them all will free the lawn of daisies.

However, in seeking to ascertain why mushrooms happen to grow in part of a lawn, it is necessary to understand that individual mushrooms are not separate independent organisms but are the fruiting bodies from an underground fungus. These fruiting bodies start, not from separate seeds, but as nodules on the mycelium: the mass of threadlike hyphae that make up the fungus. Therefore, a mushroom appears in a lawn not because a separate seed landed there but because there is a fungus in the ground which just happens to fruit in that place. Therefore, the cause of the mushrooms appearing there lies in the ground, not in the mushroom. Further, the mushrooms of the same type in the same patch of lawn are all linked, and removing each mushroom may remove the visible traces of the fungus but it will still be there and is likely to try to fruit again.

So, to understand an instance of entrepreneurship, is it relevant to look for an individual seed or for the presence in the underlying society of an entrepreneurial ethos or encouragement and how that is likely to reveal itself?

Although there are relatively few studies or reported examples which clearly identify a micro-group–level influence on entrepreneurial activity, this may be a case of the 'streetlight effect' – and the other examples outlined earlier do suggest that micro-social groups might be the right place within which to look for such an influence. The following observations would also support this view:

- It is consistent with what we know about human behaviour and the influences on it.
- Policies which try to influence individuals (i.e. which assume that the individual is the key level at which to understand and influence entrepreneurial activity) do not have the effects hoped for.
- Studies and practice in other areas have found effects at this micro-social level – for instance, studies on levels of crime, combating anti-social behaviour, young people taking up smoking and marketing fashion goods have all observed group influence.

This analysis therefore suggests that those seeking to identify and/or to influence the source of, or the main influence upon, entrepreneurial activity should look, not at individuals or at the macro-level exemplified by national conditions and policies, but at the micro-social group level and the impacts of the predominant views held in people's close social circles. These sorts of considerations are, however, only likely to be explored and considered once is it accepted that 'entrepreneurship' does not exist as the phenomenon we have supposed it to be which somehow causes people to act entrepreneurially. Thus dropping references to 'entrepreneurship' and without having it to fall back on as the supposed source of entrepreneurs and entrepreneurial activity lead to different, and possibly more accurate, perceptions of where the source of entrepreneurial activity might actually be located.

Notes

1 S. Bridge and K. O'Neill, *Understanding Enterprise, Entrepreneurship and Small Business* (Basingstoke: Palgrave Macmillan, 2013), p. 373.
2 R. Blundel and N. Lockett, *Exploring Entrepreneurship* (Oxford: Oxford University Press, 2011).
3 F. Delmar and F. C. Witte, 'The psychology of the entrepreneur', in S. Carter and D. Jones-Evans (eds), *Enterprise and Small Business* (Harlow: Pearson Education, 3rd edn, 2012), p. 152.
4 For instance in D. C. McClelland, 'Achievement Motivation Can be Developed', *Harvard Business Review*, November–December 1965, pp. 6–24.
5 R. H. Brockhaus, 'The psychology of the entrepreneur', in C. S. Kent, D. L. Sexton and K. H. Vesper (eds), *Encyclopedia of Entrepreneurship* (Englewood Cliffs, NJ, USA: Prentice Hall, 1982), p. 41.
6 Y. Gasse, commentary on R. H. Brockhaus, 'The psychology of the entrepreneur', in C. S. Kent, D. L. Sexton and K. H. Vesper (eds), *Encyclopedia of Entrepreneurship* (Englewood Cliffs, NJ, USA: Prentice Hall, 1982), p. 57.
7 S. Shane, *A General Theory of Entrepreneurship* (Cheltenham: Edward Elgar, 2003), p. 10.
8 M. Earls, *Herd: How to Change Mass Behaviour By Harnessing Our True Nature* (Chichester, UK: John Wiley & Sons Ltd, 2009), p. 95.
9 Ibid., p. 5.
10 J. Rowson, in the preface to J. Rowson and I. McGilchrist, *Divided Brain, Divided World* (London: RSA, 2013), p. 3.
11 W. J. Baumol, 'Entrepreneurship: Productive, Unproductive, and Destructive', *Journal of Political Economy*, Vol.98 No.5, pt.1, 1990, pp. 893–921.
12 P. Ball, *Critical Mass* (London: Arrow, 2004), p. 400.
13 W. J. Baumol, Op Cit.
14 E. Ní Bhrádaigh, 'Social Entrepreneurship – A Precursor to For-Profit Entrepreneurship in Peripheral Communities', paper presented at the *ICSB World Conference*, Seoul, Korea, June 2009.
15 D. B. Audretsch and M. Keilbach, *The Localization of Entrepreneurship Capital – Evidence from Germany*, Jena Economic Research Papers – ISSN 1864-7057, 2007, www.jenecon.de.

16 eg in R. Florida, *The Rise of the Creative Class* (New York: Basic Books, 2002).
17 M. Ram, G. Barrett and T. Jones, 'Ethnicity and entrepreneurship', in S. Carter S. and D. Jones-Evans (eds), *Enterprise and Small Business* (Harlow: Pearson Education, 3rd edn, 2012), p. 200.
18 S. Carter, S. Mwaura, M. Ram, K. Trehan and T. Jones, 'Barriers to Ethnic Minority and Women's Enterprise: Existing Evidence, Policy Tensions and Unsettled Questions', *International Small Business Journal*, Vol.33 No.1, 2015, pp. 49–69.
19 For instance M. Ram and D. Smallbone, *Ethnic Minority Enterprise: Policy in Practice*, Report to the Small Business Service, 2001.
20 S. Dhaliwal, *Making a Fortune – Learning from the Asian Phenomenon* (Chichester, UK: Capstone – John Wiley and Sons, 2008), p. 98.
21 M. Ram et al., Op Cit, p. 215.
22 M. Earls, Op Cit, p. 118.
23 W. J. Dennis, 'Entrepreneurship, Small Business and Public Policy Levers', *Journal of Small Business Management*, Vol.49 No.1, 2011, pp. 92–106.

8   What has produced sustained economic growth?

It has been said that 'because of the unprecedented prosperity enjoyed by the West after the Second World War, we have come to worship at the shrine of economic growth'.[1] And, in this quest for growth, entrepreneurship has been venerated for the key part it is thought to play. For instance, in 1942, not long after the term appears to have been coined, Cole spoke of entrepreneurship as being a significant feature in American economic history,[2] and then after 1979, when Birch revealed his findings about small businesses and job creation, further attention was paid to entrepreneurship as the supposed source of the businesses which would create those jobs. Therefore, as Chapter 1 indicates, 'entrepreneurship' has increasingly been seen as an, if not the, essential ingredient in economic development.

If the component assumptions of this apparent veneration of entrepreneurship are examined then it seems that it has been assumed to be the condition which leads people to become entrepreneurs, and entrepreneurs are assumed to create and/or grow businesses which will in turn deliver the jobs and economic growth sought. However, policies which have tried to deliver economic growth by stimulating entrepreneurship do not appear to have worked – which is not surprising if, as this book contends, there is not a single factor which is entrepreneurship and attempts to define it are too heterogeneous to make it a helpful concept. Therefore, it suggests, entrepreneurship does not exist as the condition it was supposed to be and we need to look elsewhere for whatever might stimulate entrepreneurs, as Chapter 7 shows, and to reassess the conditions which might actually deliver economic growth, which is considered in this chapter.

Actually the objective has probably been prosperity – and not just once-off prosperity but continuously rising levels of prosperity. However, that in turn is thought to depend on sustained economic growth with its consequent benefits of increasing tax revenues for governments and rising standards of living for those they govern. Some argue that in a planet with finite resources continuously sustained economic growth is not possible over the longer term and that sustainability should instead be the objective. However, given that the argument has not gained much ground and governments are still seeking economic growth, it might still be helpful to see what conditions might deliver such growth if 'entrepreneurship' is not the hoped-for magic answer.

The Industrial Revolution – and social development

One of the clearest sustained examples of economic growth occurred in Britain as a direct result of the Industrial Revolution. As Chapter 2 indicates, the Industrial Revolution heralded Toffler's second wave of human development. In breaking through what appears retrospectively to have been a sort of ceiling on development, it achieved a paradigm change to a state of more or less continuous growth. So the question is whether something similar can be maintained and/or repeated, and, in order to try to answer that, it is relevant to consider the conditions that led to the Industrial Revolution.

Since the agricultural revolution, noticeable growth – whether cultural, artistic, philosophic, military and/or economic – has happened on a number of occasions of which Renaissance Florence is just one example. Although it is difficult to identify exact dates for the start of such developments, Morris has suggested that for one of the most significant occasions of change, the year 1776 can be seen as a sort of symbolic turning point.[3] That was not only the year of the American Revolution and the year in which Adam Smith finished his *Wealth of Nations* and Edward Gibbon's *Decline and Fall of the Roman Empire* was published, but it was also the year in which Watt and Boulton demonstrated that their improved steam engine could pump 60 feet of water out of a mine in 60 minutes.

This demonstration of the capture and useful harnessing of energy from steam was significant because until then almost all the power applied by humans had been muscle based – from their own muscles or those of animals. More latterly some wind and water energy had been used, for instance, to move ships or turn mills, but that did not add much to the total amount of power harnessed. Steam power, however, was different, and it is estimated that by 1870 Britain's steam engines generated 4 million horsepower which is equivalent to the power output of 40 million men (who would have eaten more than Britain's annual wheat output at that time).[4]

Primitive steam engines were available in Roman times but the Romans never developed them or improved the early applications of wind and water power. Morris suggests that, before 1776, the limitations of the available sources of power had been a major constraint on social development. In order to compare on a relatively objective basis different levels of development in different societies, he has developed an index for social development[5] which is based on the four components of energy capture, urbanisation (as a proxy for organisational capacity), information processing and the capacity to make war (because more developed societies can make war more effectively – whether that is good or not). Relatively speaking, this index shows only a very slight rise from pre-history up to the Industrial Revolution. Morris's tables indicate a score of less than 10 points in 14,000 BCE rising occasionally in the last two millennia before the Industrial Revolution to only just above 40. Indeed Morris even suggests there was a sort of ceiling or threshold of around 43 points attained at times and places such as in the Roman Empire in the first century CE and in China's Song dynasty around 1100 ad[6] but not exceeded. However, the consequences of the Industrial Revolution included breaking that threshold. In Britain in 1776 the index was about 45, the highest it had been anywhere since the start of civilisation, but in the next 100 years it was to rise by 100 points and currently it is near 1000 and still rising.

Agriculture clearly played a key early role in social development. Compared to hunter-gathering it provides more secure food supplies and in denser concentrations, although, until mechanisation, it necessitated harder work over longer hours. Agriculture allowed for population increases and denser populations, but did not produce significant sustained increases in living standards – except to some extent for those at the upper levels of the stratified societies, which agriculture also facilitated. The Industrial Revolution changed that. Britain's was the first industrialisation of any national economy in the world, and the application of the term 'revolution' to this event appears first to have occurred in France where the 'revolution's' deep-seated economic changes were seen to be as fundamental as those arising from the political upheavals in the French Revolution of 1789.[7] But why did it happen when it did? As Allen puts it, explaining the Industrial Revolution has 'generated all manner of theories'[8] – and many suggestions have been made but none has been accepted conclusively as the answer.

Why was it in the West?

Diamond has attempted, in effect, to set the scene if not to answer the question directly. In his book *Guns, Germs and Steel*[9] he shows why, more or less through geographic accident, the highest stages of development happened in the West. His argument is that the advent of agriculture was a key early stage because it allowed stratified societies to evolve and those in the upper layers of such societies had the incentive and the time to invent things. Agriculture may have evolved independently in more than one centre but the people around the Fertile Crescent in the Middle East had access not only to the ancestors of some good grain crops (such as wheat, oats and barley) but also to the five best domesticable animals (horses, cows, goats, sheep and pigs) so their agriculture had the best foundation. Then the geography of the world allowed this agriculture to move east to China and West to Europe because there were similar climates all the way, and it was followed by many significant innovations[10] – both further innovations in agriculture and other innovations facilitated by that revolution, such as:

- Irrigation.
- The plough – and then the heavy plough.
- The horse collar – which allowed horses to provide the better traction needed for the heavy plough.
- The three-field system.
- Writing – an early, not directly agricultural, innovation which probably derived from a need for record keeping when food was stored centrally or communally, exchanged and/or paid in dues.
- Three-masted sailing ships – which could sail to windward. This was another non-agricultural innovation, but one which clearly preceded the Industrial Revolution.

Although, as Morris's figures suggest, the impact of agriculture on social development may have had limits, nevertheless, as Diamond describes, the agriculture that evolved in the Fertile Crescent facilitated the evolution of civilisations at various points on the east–west temperate climate band which stretches from Europe to China. Clearly the civilisation which evolved in China was very successful and many inventions were made there. Thus at one time it was ahead of Europe in this regard, but the geography of China facilitated control by a single ruling power which could enforce its will over the whole country and stop innovations if it felt so inclined. This happened, for instance, after China had developed ocean-going junks which were bigger than Columbus's ships and which reached Africa before he crossed the Atlantic. But a change at the top of the regime put in place rulers who did not like such ships and banned their use and construction – and China failed to build a wide overseas trade as a result. Europe, in contrast, had a geography which led it to be politically disunited so an innovation which might be ignored or spurned in one country could still be taken up in another and shown to work. Therefore, Diamond suggests, it was geography, not any innate characteristics of different people, which led to the ascent of the West.

Some necessary conditions

Another view is that of historians such as Mathais who has taken a more focused look at the Industrial Revolution. He notes that remarkably 'it occurred spontaneously, not being the result of conscious government policy'[11] but he also points out that, although many reasons have been suggested for its emergence, 'a very deep-seated instinct exists to look for a persuasive single-cause explanation'.[12] Among the various factors which have at one time or another been suggested as such a single cause he lists the following – along with reasons for thinking that they were not the single cause because, although they may have been necessary, they were not alone sufficient:

- *Favourable natural resources.* Clearly Britain benefitted from having streams to supply water power and conveniently located supplies of coal and iron ore. But that was all, and those resources had been there for a long time before the 18th century and were present in other countries also.
- *Protestant non-conformism.* Protestant non-conformism may have been hailed as the secret weapon of European economic growth, but it was present in other countries also, and they didn't lead the revolution.
- *A rising population.* Britain's rising population may have expanded the supply of labour and its internal market, but other countries also had rising populations but no industrial take-off.
- *A plentiful supply of capital and favourable rates of interest.* New businesses need capital at an affordable rate of interest – which was available in Britain. But Holland appears to have had lower rates of interest and more capital which had to seek investment opportunities abroad.
- *Foreign trade providing markets and wealth.* Foreign trade can provide wealth for investment and access to larger markets, but Holland had a larger foreign trade relative to the size of her economy.
- *Applied science, mechanical ingenuity and/or inventive genius.* Although scientific advance, ingenuity and invention clearly contributed to the Industrial Revolution, France arguably had as good a scientific record and higher standards of mechanical contrivance as shown, for instance, in its watch-making industry.[13]

Why in Britain – and why in the 18th century?

Thus, although the factors considered earlier may have been necessary for the Industrial Revolution to happen, none of them alone appears to explain why it happened in Britain instead of elsewhere. To try to answer this Lipsey et al. have provided an economist's view in examining the forces that appear to sustain long-term economic growth and, in particular, to explain why the West has become so rich.[14] They point out that in 1000 CE, compared to both Islam and China, Western Europe had been backward and uncivilised, yet it was because of the Industrial Revolution that in the 19th century the West achieved sustained extensive and intensive economic growth. Why then, they ask, did that revolution happen in northwest Europe, and specifically in Britain, and why did it start in the late 18th century?

Their arguments suggest that the Industrial Revolution was the product of a number of interconnected strands of development and that, in particular, at its core was the meeting between the mechanisation of textile production with the harnessing of the power of steam to drive machinery. Harnessing the power of steam depended on the application of science, which in turn involved the development, retention and transmission of scientific knowledge. Science is not just a matter of discovering new effects, but also of deducing reasons for those effects which can then, in turn, suggest new applications (see, for example, Box 8.1). As noted in earlier chapters, one of the most influential examples of this was Newton's success in bringing together strands from astronomy, mechanics, geometry and calculus to produce an explanation of gravity which enabled the previously apparently random motion of the planets to be predicted with clock-like accuracy – and the application of Newtonian mechanics was crucial for the development of the Industrial Revolution. Universities, especially those which were independent of the state, played a key role in the development, retention, transmission and application of this knowledge. Not only did they foster its acquisition through scientific questioning and empirical testing, but they also facilitated its recoding in the form of the printed word, taught it, encouraged its further dissemination and, crucially, acted as its independent custodians shielding it from any attempts to impose arbitrary state edicts.

Box 8.1   The six stages leading to a scientific understanding of magnetism

It has been said that in developing a scientific understanding of magnetism, there were six key steps. These were:

- Seeing that magnets were attracted to certain objects;
- Seeing that magnets could be used to indicate direction (compasses);
- Seeing that compasses did not always point to true north;
- Seeing that there could be local variation in compass directions;
- Seeing that compass needles tried to incline and not point horizontally;
- Forming the theory that the Earth itself is a magnet.

The Chinese, it is suggested, discovered the first two of these about the same time as the Greeks and discovered the third before the West. However, although they also knew about the fourth, they did not know the fifth and – in particular – the Chinese did not get to the sixth and crucial stage. The first five stages were essentially observations, but the sixth was the formation of a hypothesis which explained all the observations – and gave a great fillip to the understanding of magnetism.

It is also relevant to note that the discovery of the various aspects of the behaviour of compasses was both assisted by and a help to the ocean voyages which were facilitated in the West by the development of three-masted sailing ships – and prevented in China by the enforced cessation of the building and use of large ships.

Source: Informed by R. G. Lipsey, K. I. Carlaw and C. T. Bekar, *Economic Transformations* (Oxford: Oxford University Press, 2005), p. 280.

However, another factor was the influence of religious and/or state-imposed limitations on people's thinking. Some strands of Protestantism were more tolerant of new thinking as they were inclined to let people think for themselves, whereas Catholics and Muslims were encouraged to defer more to the authority of their religious texts. Galileo provided a famous example of a clash between religious dogma and new scientific thinking and, in areas where the controlling religion or state ethos was not sympathetic to new thinking, the scientific discoveries which nevertheless were made were not recognised, recorded, promulgated and/or preserved.

The two key developments suggested earlier as being at the core of the start of the Industrial Revolution are the mechanisation of textile production and the application of steam power and, of the two, it was the development of applied steam power which was dependent on scientific input because it was an understanding of the behaviours of fluids and the nature of a vacuum which suggested the potential power available from steam. In contrast it is argued that the mechanisation of textile production was more a product of trial, error and tinkering by craftsmen technicians. This mechanisation was not a new development because things like spinning wheels and simple looms were relatively early inventions, and it could be said to have been given a boost by Leonardo da Vinci. Initially this technology was used in home-based applications but, by the late 18th century, it had reached a state where factory production was advantageous because that facilitated the application of non-human power, initially from water and then from steam.

Although mechanising textile production was a process of incremental technology development requiring technological expertise, in its later stages in particular it was informed, supported and underpinned by science – the science of mechanics influenced by Newton and then of electricity as the latter allowed each machine to have its own independent engine (or engines). The development of electrical power and the science behind it were informed by observations resulting from the ocean voyages facilitated by three-masted sailing ships and compasses (as Box 8.1 indicates) because it was the scientific linking of magnetism with electricity which led to the development of the dynamo and the electric motor.

Lipsey et al. therefore identify a combination of factors such as science and mechanisation which led to the Industrial Revolution and then, in answer to the question about its location and timing, suggest that in the 18th century it was only in northwest Europe that people were developing a scientific approach to understanding and controlling the physical world and that Britain was the only country in which Newtonian mechanics were widely taught and practised. It was this understanding which facilitated the development of steam power in Britain in the late 18th century – which was where and when the steam engine met textile mechanisation and spawned the Industrial Revolution.

Would this have happened elsewhere if it had not happened in Britain? Lipsey et al. think that the Industrial Revolution could have happened in some other parts of northwest Europe, although later than in Britain, but that conditions elsewhere in the world were not suitable. For instance, of the two centres of civilisation and learning which had been so far ahead of Europe in 100 CE, neither in Islam nor China would it have been likely. Islam had been a key facilitator of knowledge acquisition, having in the 800s established a new centre of learning in Baghdad. There much Greek learning was translated into Arabic and there were many developments and discoveries. Nevertheless Islamic orthodoxy only recognised two sorts of science: Islamic science which was based on the Koran and foreign science (mainly from old Greek sources) which was useful, such as arithmetic, geometry and astrology. New thinking was not accepted as legitimate and, although it did happen to a possibly surprising extent, there was no institutional support for it and no appropriate repository for preserving such learning. As for China, it did not appear to have even the beginning of systematic cumulative modern science[15] (see Box 8.1) and had no institutional memory to preserve scientific knowledge once it was discovered. Also there was just one central government which could and did impose arbitrary decisions on everyone. Thus by the 18th century neither Islam nor China were in a good position to develop, recognise, preserve and use the scientific understanding that underlay many of the Industrial Revolution's developments. In Morris's terms both Islam and China were still trapped under the lower 40s ceiling of social development and could not break through it until the various new forms of energy capture, which the Industrial Revolution stimulated and refined, spread from the West.

And the science was crucial. Lipsey et al. distinguish two revolutions encompassing three phases of the Industrial Revolution. The first revolution, they suggest, comprised the early factory stage and the steam-driven phase in which the innovations in the leading sectors were nearly all mechanical – and most of the non-mechanical innovations in any sector were based on empirical trial and error. The second revolution, however, was the heavily science-led phase and produced innovations such as chemicals (for instance, dyes for textiles) and steel and power from electricity and the internal combustion engine – all of which required the application of fairly advanced Western scientific understanding. Thus, Lipsey et al. suggest:

> In all three phases of the Industrial Revolution, the leading sectors were the ones most influenced by science while those that were evolving purely by trial-and-error groping were lagging behind, and being pulled along by the leading sectors. Science did matter.[16]

As if to emphasise that no one view seems on its own to explain the Industrial Revolution, Allen adds another economist's view. He suggests that a crucial factor was that, compared to other countries, at that time Britain had high wage rates and low energy costs. Thus, because of Britain's high wage rates, investing in spinning jennies was a viable economic proposition because the capital cost would be recouped from the wages saved, whereas that was not the case in either France or India, two competitors in cotton production. Also, because of the very low cost of coal in Britain, it was profitable to invest in even the very inefficient early steam engines, whereas steam engines were not profitable elsewhere until they used much less fuel.[17]

The importance of an inclusive regime

So far the suggestions considered in this chapter for the causes of, or at least the conditions potentially fostering, the Industrial Revolution amount to quite a long list – but they are not all the factors suggested. Lipsey et al. include in their survey of facilitating conditions appropriate property rights because invention and innovation are risky so people will only engage in them if they think that they will secure and retain a commensurate share of any rewards that are generated.[18] Also, in his list, Mathias included a social system and government which are favourably disposed to trade and economic gain.

Both these aspects are reflected in the views of Acemoglu and Robinson who suggest that 'countries differ in their economic success because of their different institutions, the rules influencing how the economy works, and the incentives that motivate people'.[19] In particular they distinguish between the institutions they label 'inclusive' and those they label 'extractive'. By inclusive institutions, they mean those which have at their centre secure property rights and that foster economic activity, whereas extractive institutions are designed to extract income and wealth from one sub-set of society for the benefit of another, usually a ruling elite.

The reality, they report, is that countries are more likely to have extractive institutions than inclusive ones. Ancient Rome obtained its wealth by largely extractive means such as conquest and slavery. Slavery in particular is an entirely extractive system with the slave owner taking all the product of a slave's efforts and the slave being entitled to none of it – thus providing no incentive for the slave to exert himself or herself to do any more than necessary to fulfil their orders. If you expect that your property and the fruits of any extra effort or initiative on your part will be stolen, expropriated or taxed away, than you have little incentive to engage in such effort.

Conquest was what happened when the Spanish arrived in Central and South America. In effect they replaced the rulers of the various conquered people and used their acquired subjects to extract wealth for them from the country – with gold being an obvious early example. When the Spanish left and local rulers replaced them, they, too, found that the system was to their advantage and did not change it. Even revolutionaries, who may have had the best of intentions, did not bring themselves to reduce the extractive powers of government once they were the government. Extractive powers, Acemoglu and Robinson suggest, once imposed are not lightly given up.

In contrast to South America, the colonial experience of much of North America was different. Because the population densities of the Native Americans were lower than in South America, they could not be harnessed to provide labour in the same way. The only way to develop wealth from the land was to settle it, and the settlers were not going to let any authority then take away their hard-earned gains. So the United States developed inclusive institutions, even rejecting the authority of the colonial power in a revolution triggered by an attempt at 'taxation without representation'.

Ironically, according to Acemoglu and Robinson, that colonial power – England – is a country with internally one of the longest histories of inclusive institutions and an example as such to many others. Key events in its journey to inclusivity have been Magna Carta of 1215, the English Civil War between 1642 and 1651 and the Glorious Revolution of 1688 – all of which occurred because subjects were not prepared to accept the absolute power of rulers who saw themselves as being above and not subject to the law. As a result, 'England was unique among nations when it made the breakthrough to sustained economic growth in the seventeenth century'[20] and 'it is not a coincidence that the Industrial Revolution started in England a few decades after the Glorious Revolution'.[21]

Even when the benefits of the Industrial Revolution became apparent they were still resisted by some. Sustained economic growth requires innovation, which is always likely to involve an element of creative destruction – and fear of that can stimulate opposition to such developments. Thus guilds of artisans who stood to lose from the introduction of new manufacturing techniques wanted to maintain restrictive laws, and Europe provided many examples of aristocracies and elites, such as the tsarist rulers in Russia, who had very good lifestyles themselves and had a vested interest in maintaining the status quo and were thus potential losers from industrialisation. Even as late as the beginning of the 20th century the tsars were resisting factories and railways, and therefore wanted laws which restricted them, because they thought such things would encourage and facilitate workers to congregate in large groups where they might foment revolution. It is true that when the Bolsheviks took over after the Russian Revolution and enforced industrialisation, the economy of Russia grew so quickly that some others saw it as the model for the future. However, the economic gains were made by copying others and catching up and were not sustained or sustainable thereafter. The Bolshevik rule was essentially extractive and so the continuous innovation necessary to sustain growth could not flourish.

The Magna Carta could be said to have started the process in England whereby the monarch should become subject to recognised rules rather than the rules being subject to the monarch. The point was not that at the time of the Industrial Revolution the aristocracy and artisans in England did not want to maintain the status quo as their counterparts did in other countries – but that the law did not facilitate their opposition to change. Aristocratic reaction was muted, and those artisans, such as the Luddites, who attempted to destroy the new machines did not have enough support. In contrast, in countries such as Austro-Hungary and Russia, where absolutist monarchs could and did block progress, economic progress stalled even when other European nations followed the industrial lead of England. Thus, it is argued, inclusive institutions are an essential condition for sustained economic growth.

Other factors

There are also other possible factors which some authorities have suggested, two examples of which are an independent legal system and limited liability companies:

- The sort of inclusive regime identified by Acemoglu and Robinson as an essential pre-requisite for sustained economic growth is accompanied by, and dependent on, the development of a legal system which was not just a reflection of the ruler's power. A clear example of this is the US Constitution under which the legislative, executive, and judicial branches of the US government are kept distinct in order to prevent abuse of power, and so the executive cannot unilaterally dictate or otherwise order laws and judgements which reflect its wishes and interests.

- The facility for establishing a corporation as a separate legal entity from that of the individual people involved in it has also been suggested as an important means for facilitating the application of available capital to economic development. This development is referred to in Chapter 2, which also alludes to Adam Smith's opposition to it on the grounds that it would reduce the vigilance of managers. Nevertheless, as Chapter 2 also indicates, the invention of companies can be said to have made modern capitalism possible, and it would seem to have greatly facilitated the application of available wealth to fund innovative economic development. Public-sector cultures, it is said, often discourage innovation because their systems seem to be more focused on identifying fault than recognising success. Thus, because not doing something wrong is more important than doing something right, few people in the sector are prepared to take the risk of innovating and being the first to do something new in case it fails and they get the blame. In the same way few people would be prepared to invest in private-sector innovation if they are going to be held personally liable for any damage that might ensue, but the formation of limited liability companies can prevent that.

And entrepreneurship?

Thus there are factors beyond those identified in the other sources considered. However, it is noticeable that one factor which does not feature specifically in the lists and explanations summarised so far is entrepreneurship. Although it has not been entirely ignored by commentators, it has rarely been mentioned and then not as a factor in its own right – and what has been said about it has not always been consistent.

Baumol,[22] as previously noted, takes the view that there has always been entrepreneurial activity because there are entrepreneurial people in every society, but what matters is society's 'rules' about how that entrepreneurial proclivity should be used (see Box 3.1). Therefore, it will only be applied to economically productive activities, such as innovation in products and manufacturing techniques, if the relevant sections of society view such activities as socially acceptable and commendable. If they don't, then entrepreneurial people will apply their talents unproductively – for society if not for them personally – or even destructively. In terms of Dennis's diagram (see Box 7.3), did the Industrial Revolution require both institutions and culture to be positive?

Despite this apparent lack of evidence for its relevance, the assumption that entrepreneurship is linked to, and even is the key factor needed for, economic growth still persists. It has been suggested that the apparent connection between entrepreneurship and economic benefit described in Chapter 1 was readily received because the earlier contributions of McClelland had planted the idea that an entrepreneurial culture was an important driving force for economic development[23] (and see also in Chapters 3 and 5). Writing before Baumol, McClelland suggested that, in looking for the reasons for economic growth and/or decline, and despite the other reasons considered earlier, the thinking of many economists could be grouped under the headings of capital accumulation, population growth, division of labour and, he states, entrepreneurship.[24] However, he proposed that instead of combinations of these factors, the key issue was the extent to which people had a need for achievement (often referred to as *n* Achievement or *n* Ach). For McClelland this was the key factor which explained economic growth because, in order to satisfy their need for achievement, people acted entrepreneurially to build and grow new ventures. Thus entrepreneurship was involved – but only as the means by which a need for achievement resulted in economic growth.

To prove his case McClelland attempted to assess the level of the need for achievement in different societies at different periods in history by analysing their literature and showing a correlation between high-growth societies and high need for achievement measured in this way. For a time McClelland's ideas were very influential, but, subsequently, doubts emerged, and McClelland's ideas about the economic impact of a supposed need for achievement appear now largely to have been discounted.[25] Nevertheless, the link between entrepreneurship and economic growth persists in the minds of many people, albeit now without the clear foundation McClelland appeared to have provided.

Comments

> 'All happy families are alike; each unhappy family is unhappy in its own way.'
>
> Leo Tolstoy, *Anna Karenina*

Toffler's[26] first wave of development, the agricultural revolution, was itself a key factor in human economic advancement, and it led, in turn, to some significant developments and a fairly steady series of innovations. Nevertheless, progress, when it happened, was relatively slow and, although it did raise living conditions for many people, development reached a sort of plateau beyond which it seemed it could not progress. In contrast the Industrial Revolution initiated a process which appears to be more significant because it has led to a more or less continuous progression involving sustained economic growth and a significant and still continuing rise in living standards. Those governments and others who want to try to initiate a similar boost and/or sustain economic growth want to achieve similar effects – and thus want to establish which factors are necessary for that boost. Therefore, a key question for those seeking to start or maintain that sort of economic development is what were the Industrial Revolution's antecedents, necessary conditions, causes and/or triggers?

However, it has been suggested that 'to pose the question of what needs to happen before self-sustained economic growth can develop is to search for a Holy Grail',[27] and this chapter does not claim to have found one. Instead, from examining various accounts of economic development in general and the Industrial Revolution in particular, it has identified a wide range of suggestions for contributing conditions, none of which alone appears to be sufficient, but all, or almost all, of which may have been necessary and often not separately but inter-linked. Clearly the consequences of the Industrial Revolution for Britain, and then for those countries which adopted the same methods, included rises in both economic output and standards of living. However, it would seem that many factors contributed to the Industrial Revolution happening when and where it did and therefore, as most, if not all, of those factors seemed to have been necessary, there are many reasons why it didn't happen at another time and in another place. Like Anna Karenina's unhappy families, the circumstances of the Industrial Revolution appear to be very special and to require the conjunction of so many conditions – with the result that the many economies which failed to meet these requirements can each appear to have failed in a different way. And just catching up with what others are doing is not the same thing – as the example of Stalinist Russia shows. Getting and staying ahead requires different factors.

A further relevant observation from the analysis in this chapter is that entrepreneurship does not emerge as a relevant factor. It is not on the lists of essential conditions suggested by any of the authorities consulted. Baumol mentioned it, but suggests that it is always present and that what matters instead is how it is used, which, he suggests, depends on social norms. McClelland also mentioned it, but as the link between *n* Achievement and economic growth rather than as a primary factor in its own right and, in any case as indicated earlier, many now discount McClelland's ideas.

Is it the case that, in seeking to explain why the Industrial Revolution occurred when and where it did, we more readily recognise and/or value the factors from our own disciplines? Thus many who want economic growth are economists who will tend to see, or at least to seek, economic reasons for the Industrial Revolution and ignore human ones such as society's rules and other aspects of the cultural dimension, whereas others may ignore economic factors in favour of their own specialities. Have we also swung too much towards a reliance on left-brained, clock-like thinking? Newton's rigorous, deterministic approach was an essential contribution to the development of scientific thinking, but have we become too wedded to the idea that if we look hard enough, we will find a clear deterministic cause for any effect we seek to explain? Clearly we have not found a clear, deterministic and repeatable cause of the Industrial Revolution, but is that because we still have not looked hard enough or because no such cause exists? In particular this study has not identified entrepreneurship in any form as such a deterministic cause, so should we abandon our assumptions about its efficacy?

Overall a conclusion from this study is that there is no immediately obvious prescription for sustained economic growth, other than trying to ensure that all the factors mentioned earlier are present. Also, in particular, this exercise does not identify an injection of 'entrepreneurship' as a sufficient, or even as a necessary, contributory cause, although ensuring that all the factors are present might deliver the conditions which encourage and/or allow entrepreneurs to emerge and to flourish.

Productive entrepreneurs do appear to have been part of the Industrial Revolution, and these entrepreneurs started businesses which created wealth and employed people. But if we only look at those businesses or at the people (entrepreneurs) who created them, we will miss the reasons why the Industrial Revolution occurred where and when it did. Entrepreneurs are not identified in the previous analysis as a key factor. Is it therefore the case that, instead of being one of the factors that needed to be in place for the Industrial Revolution to happen, productive entrepreneurial activity in any form was something that happened when the relevant factors all came together? Instead of being an ingredient which could be added to create the conditions necessary, was it actually created by those conditions? Was it a product of the process, not a cause of it?

Notes

1 L. Siedentop, *Inventing the Individual* (London: Penguin, 2015), p. 2.
2 A. H. Cole, 'Entrepreneurship as an Area of Research', *The Journal of Economic History*, Vol.2 supplement, 1942, pp. 118–126.
3 See I. Morris, *Why the West Rules – For Now* (London: Profile Books, 2011), pp. 490–497.

4 Ibid., p. 497.
5 Ibid., pp. 147–149.
6 Ibid., p. 168.
7 P. Mathias, *The First Industrial Nation* (London: Methuen, 1983), p. 3.
8 R. C. Allen, *The British Industrial Revolution in Global Perspective* (Cambridge: Cambridge University Press, 2009), p. 3.
9 J. Diamond, *Guns, Germs and Steel* (London: Vintage, 1998).
10 R. G. Lipsey, K. I. Carlaw and C. T. Bekar, *Economic Transformations* (Oxford: Oxford University Press, 2005).
11 P. Mathias, Op Cit, p. 4.
12 Ibid., p. 7.
13 Ibid., pp. 7–11.
14 R. G. Lipsey et al.
15 Ibid., Op Cit, p. 278.
16 Ibid., p. 254.
17 R. C. Allen, Op Cit.
18 R. G. Lipsey et al., Op Cit, p. 68.
19 D. Acemoglu and J. A. Robinson, *Why Nations Fail* (London: Profile Books, 2013), p. 73.
20 Ibid., p. 102.
21 Ibid., p. 103.
22 W. Baumol, 'Entrepreneurship: Productive, Unproductive, and Destructive', *Journal of Political Economy*, Vol.98 No.5, pt.1, 1990.
23 S. Beugelsdijk and R. Smeets, 'Entrepreneurial Culture and Economic Growth: Revisiting McClelland's Thesis', *American Journal of Economics and Sociology*, Vol.67 No.5, 2008, pp. 915–916.
24 D. C. McClelland, *The Achieving Society* (Princeton, NJ: D. Van Nostrand Company Inc., 1961), p. 9.
25 For instance S. Beugelsdijk and R Smeets, Op Cit, pp. 915–939.
26 A. Toffler, *The Third Wave* (London: Collins, 1980).
27 P. Mathias, Op Cit, p. 6.

9   To conclude

Distinguishing myth from reality

Since the term entrepreneurship was first coined, it is clear that most, if not all, of those who have used the word have believed that it referred to something real. However, this book suggests, the search for that reality has produced more questions than answers.

The meaning of words

> 'When I use a word,' Humpty Dumpty said in rather a scornful tone, 'it means just what I choose it to mean – neither more nor less.'
>
> 'The question is,' said Alice, 'whether you *can* make words mean so many different things.'
>
> 'The question is,' said Humpty Dumpty, 'which is to be master – that's all.'
>
> Lewis Carroll, *Through the Looking-Glass,*
> *and What Alice Found There* (1871)

Words have been important in the search for entrepreneurship. Without words for entrepreneurs and entrepreneurship, there would have been no search for them, and part of that search has been attempts, through proposed definitions, to agree on the meaning of those words – not least in order to provide a clear focus for the search. But can we rely on the meaning of words? If we have a word for something, does that mean that the thing exists and that our word for it refers specifically to it?

Chapter 1 quotes a remark from a vice-president of the International Council for Small Business (ICSB) who, writing in 1992, noted that there had been a recent dramatic increase in the literature about entrepreneurship and commented that the evolution of entrepreneurship as an academic field was 'a positive movement toward a commonly accepted definition of entrepreneurship and toward the definition of the boundaries of the field of entrepreneurship'.[1] Thus, a decade after entrepreneurship had started to become such a popular subject, there seemed to be a clear perception that entrepreneurship existed as an identifiable and definable phenomenon, the nature of which was being revealed by exploration and research – a perception which still continues today in some quarters.

This perception may, at least in part, have come from a common expectation that, if we have a word for something, it must refer to a specific identifiable thing that exists (or used to exist). As one commentator has observed 'the idea that a language is a list of names for things that exist runs through Western thought'.[2] However, the reality is much more complex. For instance, we do use some words for things that many of us think do not exist (or have not yet been shown to exist), such as 'ghost' and 'levitation', and we have words with different uses which refer to more than one thing that exists. Take the word 'head'. It can refer to that part of a person's body which sticks out at the top or to the part of an animal or insect which sticks out at the front. However, it is also used to defer to a piece of land which sticks out into the sea, to the foam at the top of a pint of beer or to the person at the top of an organisation. These meanings may have come from the same source but they refer to different things – and are represented in French by different words such as *tête*, *cap*, *mousse* and *chef* or *patron*.[3]

To quote one authority, it is clear that 'the semantics of words is an intellectual mess'[4] and the idea that one word should have one meaning is very misleading. At least one person has observed that much of the world's troubles could be ascribed to the illusion that a thing exists just because we have a word for it.[5] Nevertheless the assumption that words are invented as labels for observed phenomena leads to the conclusion that, if we have a word for something, it must exist. Further, this assumption appears to have affected our view of entrepreneurship, not least when we presume that all uses of the word must be referring to the same real thing or at least to aspects of it. Thus we often appear to assume that all references to 'entrepreneurs' and 'entrepreneurship' are as consistent and as specific as references to 'Australia' and 'Australian' (see Box 9.1).

Box 9.1 The differing concepts of Australia and Germany

Just because we have a concept of something, that is not a guarantee that it exists or, if it does exist, that it has a single unique identity. For instance, we now have a clear concept of Australia and what it is, but this was not always the case. As far back as Roman times there was the concept of a legendary Southern land which even had a name: *Terra*

Australis Incognita or 'unknown land of the South'. Although it was first populated by humans between 40,000 and 50,000 years ago, the first recorded visit by Europeans was only just over 400 years ago when the Dutch made landfall in 1606 and later charted the north and west coasts. In 1770 James Cook mapped the east coast and, after the establishment of a British colony in 1788 in Sydney, the interior was also eventually explored and mapped. Thus, although earlier for Europeans its position and even existence had not been clear, today Australia's location and extent are objectively distinguishable and its boundaries are not challenged or changing.

But can the same be said of our concept of Germany? The area we now know as Germany is a part of northwestern Europe which largely resisted the Roman Empire, but much of it later became part of what was known somewhat ironically as the Holy Roman Empire. The extent of this latter empire fluctuated, but at its largest extent it spread from the Baltic to Italy and from Burgundy to Bohemia, including the area we have been accustomed to refer to as Germany. Many of the people in the 'Empire' may have spoken a Germanic language but it was not a single county and included several large and many small separate political units, often with their own distinct histories.

After many changes, including the two separate states of East and West Germany, there is now a clear boundary for the current state of Germany, but it does not include all German-speaking peoples, such as those of Austria and part of Switzerland. It does not include what was the oldest university in the Germanic world, which was in Prague, or the home of the German philosopher Immanuel Kant, who was born and lived in Königsberg (which is now Kaliningrad and a part of Russia), or the German city with its Gothic Cathedral which so inspired Goethe, which was Strasbourg. So, as Goethe wrote of Germany in 1796: 'I don't know where to find such a country', and as one modern author puts it, 'in Germany both geography and history have always been unstable'.[6]

Therefore, although Australia has existed as a distinct continent for longer than humans have been a distinct species, initially our Eurocentric concept of it was as an unknown land somewhere in the south, and its existence and extent have only relatively recently been clarified. In the case of Germany, although there has been a concept of it since Roman times and its existence has not been in doubt, what has changed is just how much of Europe we have thought of as being German and the extent of the recognised state or states that have officially comprised it.

Connections real and apparent

It is not unknown for science and/or exploration and discovery to find a link between different apparently unconnected things, or to find that some similarly labelled things are not related, or that some clearly identified and named things do not exist:

- Caterpillars and butterflies behave very differently but are closely related, and drab cygnets do turn into handsome swans.
- Goose barnacles, however, do not turn into barnacle geese. (At one time, before the migration of birds was understood, it was a mystery in temperate Europe where barnacle geese appeared from each winter, because they disappeared again before the summer and were never seen to nest. Therefore, it was supposed that they came from goose barnacles probably because of their similar colour and shape.)
- The 'lead' in pencils is not the element lead but largely graphite, which is dark, opaque and a good conductor of electricity. In contrast diamonds are clear, highly transparent and poor conductors of electricity. But we now know that graphite and diamonds are both carbon, as also are coal, soot and graphine.
- When light was shown to act like a wave, the concept of a universal *luminiferous aether* was suggested as the medium through which those waves were propagated. However, experiments were never able to detect it and eventually other theories of light were advanced which did not need it.
- Australia is a concept which has evolved from just a supposition that there might be a southern continent to its discovery as a definable, concrete reality (see Box 9.1). Utopia, however, has not been found. It is the name coined by Sir Thomas More as the concept of a near-perfect or ideal community or society, and Erewhon is a country invented by Samuel Butler in his eponymous book. Both are fictional and however much we might wish for Utopia, it doesn't exist.

The power of a dominant paradigm

A long habit of not thinking something is WRONG, gives it a superficial appearance of being RIGHT, and raises at first a formidable outcry in defence of custom.

Thomas Paine

It ain't what you don't know that gets you into trouble. It's what you know for sure that just ain't so.

Mark Twain

Has a continued belief in the concept of entrepreneurship, reinforced by the continuing use of the word, prevented us from seeing some of the reality of this aspect of the world of work? Is this what Daniel Kahneman, the Nobel laureate, called theory-induced blindness?

> Once you have accepted a theory and used it as a tool in your thinking, it is extraordinarily difficult to notice its flaws. If you come upon an observation that does not seem to fit the model, you assume that there must be a perfectly good explanation that you are somehow missing. You give the theory the benefit of the doubt, trusting the community of experts who have accepted it. . . . As the psychologist Daniel Gilbert observed, disbelieving is hard work.[7]

Has our thinking about entrepreneurship been influenced by a particular train of thought: a paradigm? The *Oxford English Dictionary* defines 'paradigm' as 'a pattern or example',[8] and it was Kuhn, in his analysis of scientific revolutions,[9] who used this word in the context of scientific thought and introduced the term 'paradigm shift' to refer to the revolutionary change which happens when one prevailing scientific view gives way to another.

That change is necessary when, in the light of new or newly recognised evidence, a previously dominant view or paradigm no longer appears to be justified, and hence there is a shift to a new paradigm. However, until that happens, the dominant paradigm has a considerable influence on the way that thinking in that area is focused and structured. As Kuhn indicates, because the student in such a scientific field joins people who

> learned the bases of their field from the same concrete models, his (or her) subsequent practice will seldom evoke overt disagreement over fundamentals. Men whose research is based on shared paradigms are committed to the same rules and standards of scientific practice.[10]

As an example of how a 'dominant paradigm' exerts its influence, the Wikipedia entry for 'paradigm' suggests that

> the following are conditions that facilitate a system of thought to become an accepted dominant paradigm:
>
> * Professional organisations that give legitimacy to the paradigm
> * Dynamic leaders who introduce and purport the paradigm
> * Journals and editors who write about the system of thought. They both disseminate the information essential to the paradigm and give the paradigm legitimacy

- Government agencies who give credence to the paradigm
- Educators who propagate the paradigm's ideas by teaching it to students
- Conferences conducted that are devoted to discussing ideas central to the paradigm
- Media coverage
- Lay groups, or groups based around the concerns of lay persons, that embrace the beliefs central to the paradigm
- Sources of funding to further research on the paradigm.[11]

Most, if not all, of these conditions apply to the field of entrepreneurship and to thinking about and researching it in recent years. So to what extent has the search for entrepreneurship been affected by, or been the manifestation of, a dominant paradigm – and what blinkers has that dominant paradigm put on our thinking? Has it, for instance, led us:

- To use the wrong models? Has our thinking been based too much on business as the model for entrepreneurship and on big business as the proper business model?
- To use the wrong thinking? Has our approach been too left-brained and not sufficiently right-brained and our thinking too clock-like and not cloud friendly?
- To ignore key influences? Have we been too ignorant of factors such as the social nature of human behaviour and of ideas such as the different effects of inclusive or extractive institutions?

The half-life of knowledge

The impact of seeing things from different perspectives, viewing them, for instance, as clouds not clocks or with the right side of the brain instead of the left, can often lead us to reject, or at least to question, some long-established assumptions. As Galbraith explained, when considering conventional wisdom:

> Economic and social behavior are complex, and to comprehend their character is mentally tiring. Therefore we adhere, as though to a raft, to those ideas which represent our understanding.[12]

Upsetting this conventional wisdom is therefore frequently uncomfortable – but nevertheless sometimes needs to be done if new ideas are to emerge. A concept which embraces this is that of the half-life of knowledge which, for any particular field of study, is the period of time after which 50 per cent of the current knowledge in that field is likely to be shown to be incorrect and/or superseded because it is either wrong or irrelevant. It is not generally a question of whether the knowledge in a subject has a half-life, but only of how long that half-life is. Half-lives appear to be long in basic subjects like physics, although the way that Einstein's interpretation of gravity has replaced Newton's shows that there is change even there, and mathematics may be the exception with an infinite half-life. But the half-lives of knowledge in applied sciences like medicine are clearly short – indeed in psychology it is said to be as little as 5 years. So what is the half-life of knowledge likely to be in the field of entrepreneurship, which, if it is a science, is also an applied one?

The concept of the half-life of knowledge suggests that, in any subject, and not least entrepreneurship, it should be expected that parts of current wisdom will, sooner or later, be shown to be wrong. That is not the fault of the 'experts' in the subject for getting it wrong but is an inevitable part of the exploration and experimentation that are necessary for eventually getting things right. It does, however, mean that new and/or different perspectives, which can help to highlight where revision might be due, should not be ignored and shunned but should be sought out and welcomed.

Rethinking entrepreneurship

It is clear that we have had a concept to which the label 'entrepreneurship' has been applied, even though we can't all agree on what it is. Then, apparently on the assumption that there is no smoke without fire, the widespread use of the word entrepreneurship appears somehow to have led us to believe that there must be a reality behind the concept.

The analysis in this book indicates that we have supposed entrepreneurship to be a condition which not only explains why people become entrepreneurs, but also is deterministic because it will respond to influences in predictable ways. Further, because we have believed that entrepreneurs deliver economic growth, we have wanted to have more of them – and have therefore sought to identify that deterministic condition so that we can use it to get more entrepreneurs. But we haven't found it – instead of a clear identifiable condition, we have found just mixed and contradictory meanings of entrepreneurship with no definitive unity.

Further, the supposed existence of entrepreneurship has led to errors such as looking for the source of entrepreneurial activity in the wrong place and seeing such activity as a condition necessary for economic growth instead of being the result of such conditions. In general it has only served to:

- Confuse – because of its mixed meanings;
- Mislead – because it implies a condition which does not exist;

- Misdirect – because it has led us to look in the wrong place for the things we do want.

This indicates that entrepreneurship is an invented concept and a myth – and is very unhelpful. Therefore, we should abandon the concept and stop using the word.

Notes

1 G. R. Plaschka, ICSB Senior Vice President for Research and Publication, writing in the *Bulletin of the International Council for Small Business* Vol.24 No.1, Winter 1992.
2 D. Bellos, *Is That a Fish in Your Ear?* (London: Penguin, 2012), p. 83.
3 Based on comments in D. Bellos, Op Cit, pp. 85–86.
4 D. Bellos, Op Cit, p. 87.
5 C. K. Ogden quoted in D. Bellos, *Is That a Fish in Your Ear?* (London: Penguin, 2012), p. 21.
6 N. MacGregor, *Germany: Memories of a Nation* (London: Allen Lane, 2014).
7 D. Kahneman, *Thinking, Fast and Slow* (London: Penguin Group, 2011), p. 277.
8 *The Compact Edition of the Oxford English Dictionary* (Oxford: Oxford University Press, 1971).
9 T. S. Kuhn, *The Structure of Scientific Revolutions* (Chicago: University of Chicago, 1962).
10 Ibid., 3rd edn, 1996, p. 11.
11 Wikipedia, *Paradigm*, https://en.wikipedia.org/wiki/Paradigm (accessed 5 August 2015).
12 J. K. Galbraith, *The Affluent Society*, first published in USA 1958 (London: Penguin: 4th edn, 1991), p. 6.

Index

Note: Page numbers in italic indicate a figure, table, or box on the corresponding page.